**Skylarks and Seagulls**

# Buttercups and Brambles

## Children of Portlethen

Elizabeth A Dodds

Published in 2017

with the help of Lumphanan Press

9 Anderson Terrace, Tarland,

Aberdeenshire, AB34 4YH


www.lumphananpress.co.uk

Printed and bound by Imprint Digital,

Upton Pyne, Devon, UK


ISBN:  978-0-9935971-8-3

# Contents

For Ellen, James, Phoebe and Matthew
and all the little children in the family

# Introduction

In 1939, the same year that saw the outbreak of World War II, my parents married and came to live in Portlethen. They had met a few years earlier in the Shetland Islands, finding their way there from very different backgrounds and by very different routes.

My father, Alexander Dunn, was an only child, born and raised in the town of Beith in Ayrshire where his father worked as a furniture designer. He was a clever lad and won a scholarship to Glasgow University, the first person in his family ever to go to University. There he studied Latin, Greek and Hebrew, took a Theology degree, qualified as a Church of Scotland minister and chose to spend his probationary year as minister of the parish of Northmavine in the Shetland Isles.

My mother, Florence Hourston, was born on the farm of Ploverhall in Evie, Orkney, the tenth child in a family of fourteen children. She went to the local school where the sole teacher, Billy Anderson, taught all the children in a single classroom. She left school when she was 14 years old with no qualifications, stayed at home on the farm helping her mother until she was 17, and then took the boat and the train to Glasgow to enrol as a student nurse at the Sick Children's Hospital and later at the Western Infirmary. There she flourished and with hard work, ability and sheer determination ended up as the top student in her year with medals in both medical and surgical nursing. She moved from Glasgow to Edinburgh to complete her Queen's District Nurse training before being sent as district nurse to Northmavine in Shetland.

When our father was appointed minister of Portlethen, my parents moved into the Manse and, with a blend of our Dad's gentle idealism and our Mum's stalwart pragmatism, set about turning it into a warm, loving family home. In 1941 my brother, Stuart, was born. I followed in 1942, my sister, Marilyn, in 1944 and Sandra in 1947. All of us were born at home in the years before the founding of the NHS (National Health Service) that came into effect in July 1948. There was no free ante-natal care but Dr Horne was on call day and night and attended all our births. After the doctor had left, we were handed over into the capable hands of our Aunt Nettie, Mum's older sister, who was a qualified nurse and midwife. She looked after us for a week or so while Mum rested in bed, as was the accepted practice following childbirth in these days.

We were born into a world at war and grew up in its shadow. Reminders of the 1939-45 War were all around us: there were anti-tank concrete blocks on the cliff top at Portlethen shore, radar pylons and a RAF station on the horizon at Craighead, bombed out buildings round the docks in Aberdeen. People told stories of German planes flying overhead, of sirens and blackout curtains, of the very real fear of invasion. Rationing was still in place throughout our childhood. If anyone wanted to buy clothes or food they had to hand over their ration book to the shopkeeper who would tear out the appropriate number of coupons before handing the book back. We were lucky because each child was given their own ration book, allowing families like ours with children to buy extra food and clothes. In addition, all pre-school infants had an allowance of orange juice and cod-liver oil malt, and all school children were given a bottle of milk to drink every morning at break.

It was a time of food shortages in the country, when everyone with a garden was encouraged to "dig for victory," uprooting the rose bushes and lawns, replanting with crops that could be eaten. Like most families in Portlethen, we grew our own vegetables and fruit in the garden, adding to the store of jams and jellies by going bramble picking along the hedgerows in the autumn. With the produce from the garden and the constant supply of eggs from our hens, we in The Manse were fortunate and never went hungry.

However, we were aware that Portlethen had been sheltered from the worst effects of the War. Children living in London, or Glasgow or Cardiff had experienced a very different War with their houses bombed to smithereens, their streets and schools reduced to rubble. Many of the men we knew in Portlethen were either too old for active service or were in "reserved occupations," like the farmers, the doctors, the teachers or the ministers, like our Dad. I was not aware of any child in my class who had lost a father in the War, and yet there are ten names of men who died in the 1939-45 War on the Memorial outside the church on top of the hill.

This was a time when there were hardships compared to today's modern world: we had to keep the house warm in winter without central heating, to clean floors and carpets without a vacuum cleaner, to wash clothes, sheets and blankets without a washing machine or tumble drier, to keep food fresh without refrigerators and freezers, to shop for groceries without supermarkets, to entertain ourselves without television or computers. It was a time when children were expected to do what they were told by their parents without any arguments and to obey and respect their teachers at school, to work hard in class and learn the skills they would need to earn a living.

Growing up in Portlethen at that time, we accepted these hardships because we knew nothing different. What we did know was that there had been a War and that we had won. Our troubles were now over: we wouldn't all have to learn to speak German. We were living in a country and a community that felt safe and, if we worked hard, we could do anything we wanted in life. I remember a happy childhood in Portlethen at a time when everyone was optimistic and full of confidence that the future would be a lot brighter than the past.

The stories in this book give a view of life in Portlethen at this particular time, seen through the eyes of the children in one family. I have written them for my brother and sisters, for the children in our family and for all the people who knew my parents. I have also written them for everyone who lives in Portlethen now and would like to know something of the history of this very special community.

*Elizabeth Dodds (nee Dunn)*
*9th July, 2017*

# Acknowledgements

These stories are a record of my own memories together with those of my brother and sisters and I want to thank Stuart Dunn, Marilyn Stronach and Sandra Edwards for their contributions. I must say a particular thank you to Marilyn for casting her teacher's eye over the text and editing it for me, and to Stuart Dunn and John Edwards for drawing a plan of the farm of Balquharn which played a significant part in our childhood.

I also want to thank three of my former classmates at Portlethen Primary School, Alasdair Grant, Sandy Moir and Kathleen Boyne (nee Milne) for their help in reminding me of the names of children in our class photograph. I apologize to those we have forgotten and would appreciate anyone helping us fill in the blanks. Kathleen and I have spent hours reminiscing about the old days and I want to take the opportunity of acknowledging the support offered to our family in the Manse by the Milne family in Gushetneuk during our time in Portlethen.

My thanks also go to Jacqui Harbour (nee Wright) for her memories of Mrs Thompson's Shop and to Joy Goodlad and Christine De Luca, two members of the Pearson family who came to stay with us each summer, for their help with the story about "The Shetlanders." Christine has given me permission to reproduce her lovely poem, "Pilgrimage to Portlethen," published in her book of poetry entitled "Plain Song."

I am grateful to Allan Dodds for his help with the photographs in this book and to Glen Ross of the Colours Gallery in Edinburgh for allowing me to use a detail of "Harvesting in East Lothian," painted in 1906 by Robert Noble, for the cover. Thank you also to

Fiona Coutts (nee Wood) and Ronald Stark, two of our classmates at Mackie Academy, for their offer of information and photographs of Stonehaven Swimming Pool.

My thanks also go to friends here in Nottingham, particularly Jean, Susan, Margaret, Ian, Judith, Trish, Elvire and Christine, and to my children, Jenny and Jonathan, for their constant support and encouragement.

A very special Thank You goes to the children of Portlethen Primary School and Fishermoss Primary School. In November 2015, just after the publication of "Skylarks and Seagulls," Marilyn and I were invited to come into the schools, read some of our stories, talk to the children and answer questions about what it was like to live in Portlethen when we were their age. They wanted to know how we managed to buy food when there was no Asda Supermarket and no take-away fish and chip shops. They asked why I hadn't written about my schooldays and wanted to know more about the animals we kept as pets and how we spent our free time when there was no television and no Internet. One little boy from Mrs Sayer's class in Fishermoss asked if I'd written any other books and when I said, No, this was my first, he observed, with the blunt honesty of a child, that in that case I wasn't a "real " author and certainly not famous. So, in an effort to answer their questions and with the hope I might now be considered a "real" author, I have written this second collection of stories about the lives of children in Portlethen in the years just after the War, while it was still a small farming community and before the coming of the oil industry.

# January

Stuart and Elizabeth Dunn at Portlethen Primary School

# Schooldays

We're standing at the back gate of the Manse waiting for Kathleen and Sandy Milne from Gushetneuk to come and walk with us to school. It's a cold, frosty morning and I button up my coat and stamp my feet to try and keep warm. I watch my brother, Stuart, tapping the ice on the puddles with his tackety boots, and listen to the sharp crack as the surface splits into a thousand jagged pieces. I see my little sister, Marilyn, reach out her hand to catch a falling snowflake on her woollen mitten. I tuck my long pigtails under the hood of my coat and wish Kathleen and Sandy would hurry up.

Suddenly, there's the sound of a banging door and a slamming gate and down the road they come, slipping and sliding, hurrying to join us. We walk together down the Manse Road, round the Post Office corner and join the crowd of children making their way past the Jubilee Hall, along Station Road, turning in through the gates of Portlethen School. The playground is full of noisy, boisterous children, pushing and shoving, screaming and shouting at each other. I used to find it frightening when I first started but now I'm used to it and know how to keep out of trouble.

At exactly 9 o'clock, we hear the clanging of a bell and out onto the step at the front of the school comes the Headmaster, Mr Little, swinging a large brass bell in his hand, just like the town crier in stories of olden days. We run to form up in lines, one for each class, girls at the front, boys at the back. Marilyn is in the first line on the left with the other Primary One children. I'm in the Primary Three line. Stuart's is in the row along with the Primary Four class. Mr Little stands waiting until everyone is in place, facing him, silent and still.

"Good Morning, children," he says, peering at us through round, steel-rimmed spectacles.

"Good Morning, Mr Little," we chorus in reply.

The Headmaster waves his hand and the little children in Primary One walk forward and file in through the front door of the School, followed by Primary Two. Then it's our turn and I follow my friends, Kathleen Milne and Linda McKay, into the cloakroom where we hang our coats on the pegs, pick up our schoolbags and make our way into the classroom.

Miss Duncan, our teacher, is standing beside her desk in front of the blackboard, smiling to welcome us. I notice that there's a fire blazing in the grate in the corner of the room and beside it a scuttle full of coal. This is unusual: it's only in very cold weather that they light the fire. I take my seat at a double desk, next to one of the tall windows, along the far wall and Kathleen slides in next to me. I open my schoolbag, take out my pencil case and set out a pencil and rubber in the groove at the top of the desk. I take out two exercise books, one for Arithmetic, one for English, my Reading book and my Arithmetic textbook, lift the lid of the desk and lay them inside, ready for later. All the children are doing the same and when we're finished we sit up straight and fold our arms.

We start every day with the Register. Miss Duncan calls out our names, one by one, and we answer, "Present." If there is silence, the teacher looks up, says the name again and, if no one answers, she puts an "O" in her register to mark that child "Absent." When she's finished she closes the Register and puts it away in her desk drawer.

Next, we practise our Times Tables. The teacher starts us off, and then we chant together,

"Two ones are two, two twos are four, two threes are six, all the way to two twelves are twenty four."

Then we chant the Three Times Table, and the Four Times Table until we reach the Twelve Times Table. The Twelve Times Table is quite difficult but we need to know it because there are twelve pennies in a shilling, twelve inches in a foot and twelve items in a dozen.

Once we've finished chanting our Tables, it's time for Mental Arithmetic. Sometimes the teacher goes round the class, one at a time. I get a bit nervous when I know it's my turn next but, because we've practised it day after day, I always get it right. At other times, she asks a question and you have to shoot your hand up as soon as you know the answer.

"What's nine times six?"

"What's eight times seven?"

"How many pennies are there in six shillings?"

"How many eggs are there in five dozen?"

"How many inches are there in three feet?"

Just as we're finishing our Mental Arithmetic, there's a knock on the classroom door and in comes the Janitor, carrying a crate of milk bottles. He tries to move quietly so as not to disturb us but we're curious and watch as he lays the milk crate down in front of the fire. We can see that some of the cardboard tops are bulging up into domes while others seem to have popped off altogether leaving little igloos of ice sticking out of the bottles.

Primary 1 and 2 at Portlethen Primary School, 1947

(for pupil list see Appendix 2)

"The tops are frozen," says the Janitor to Miss Duncan. "They'll need to sit by the fire a while till they thaw out."

"Thank you, Mr Laing," says the teacher.

The Janitor tips up the scuttle and throws a bit more coal onto the fire, then turns and leaves the room.

Miss Duncan calls our attention back to our work. She tells us to get out our exercise books, the ones with squares that we use for sums, and our Arithmetic textbook and to turn to page 52. She shows us on the blackboard how to do the first sum, and then we have to practise by completing all the sums on the page. The teacher walks around the classroom, helping the children who are finding it difficult. Sometime the sums are simple addition or sub-traction, multiplication or division. Sometimes we have to add up columns of pounds, shillings and pence or answer questions like,

"If you go to the shop and buy 3 bars of chocolate at 6 pence a bar, how much change would you get from half a crown?"

When we've finished all the sums on the page, Miss Donald collects in our exercise books so that she can mark them.

Now it's Break Time and Alasdair Grant, who is the "Milk Monitor" this week, carries the crate of milk from the fireplace and sets it down on the floor near the teacher's desk. The rest of us queue up and Alasdair hands us a bottle of milk and a straw. We take them back to our desk, poke a hole in the centre of the cardboard top, stick the straw in and suck up the milk. When the bottle is empty, we prise off the top, turn it over and lick the cream that is lurking underneath. Usually we put the empty bottle back in the crate and the straw and top in the bin but today I'm going to keep my cardboard top and take it home to make a pompom.

It's quite easy making a pompom. You stick two bottle tops together, then loop round all the odd bits of wool left over from knitting cardigans and jumpers. You thread the wool through the hole in the middle and round the outside, and then back through the hole till it's tightly filled. Next you cut the wool round the edges, tie all the bits together in the middle, remove the cardboard and you're left with a fluffy, woollen pompom, just the thing for kittens to play with or for decorating pencil cases or babies' prams.

When everyone in the class has finished their milk, we can go out to play for quarter of an hour. We always have to go outside at break time, even on days when it's cold and bucketing rain. Today it's not raining but it is freezing cold, and so we fetch our coats and gloves from the cloakroom. Me and Kathleen run across the playground to the metal bars at the school gate, climb on the bottom bar and do a somersault over the top bar. Over and over we go, roly-poly, tumbling again and again till I start to feel a bit dizzy. I stop and sit on the top bar, legs dangling, and look around the playground. I can see Marilyn playing tag with her little friends, chasing each other, shouting when they catch someone. I can see a group of older girls skipping, "double ropies", with a girl at each end cawing the ropes. I can hear them chanting, jumping in time to the words,

"Jelly on a plate

Jelly on a plate

Wibble wobble, wibble wobble

Jelly on a plate."

I've been learning how to skip "double ropies." It's quite difficult because you've got to remember to jump zigzag over the two ropes as they come at you from either side.

On the other side of the playground I can see Stuart and his pals have made a slide on the icy surface and are running, then launching themselves, crouching down on their haunches, whizzing along till they reach the gravel near the wall and skidding to a stop. I can see Mr Laing, the janitor, filling up a bucket with sand ready to throw over the ice the minute we go inside. I wonder if he's forgotten how much fun a slide is for children because now he sees it only as a nuisance.

In the distance I hear the school bell ringing, and just have time for one more somersault over the bar before we all troop back inside to hang up our coats and go back to our classrooms.

Now it's time for Reading and Writing. I open my desk and take out my Reading Book - it's called "Radiant Reading. Book 1. Sunbeams." Miss Duncan says,

"Open your Reading Book at page twenty five," and then she asks,

"Can anyone read the title of today's story?"

Lots of hands shoot up. The teacher waits a little while to give everyone a chance to try to read the words before choosing someone.

"Yes, Sheena."

"The Swallow's Holiday," answers Sheena Crockett.

The teacher writes the word "swallow" on the blackboard with her chalk and underlines the letter "a." She tells us that, although it is pronounced as if it was an "o", it is a spelt with an "a". At the beginning of each story in our Reading Book there is always a section called "Words" where it lists words we may not have come across before. One of the words today is "hollow", which sounds the same as "swallow" but this time is spelt with an "o". I don't think it's fair that some words follow the rules and others don't. It's no wonder we find it hard to learn to read and spell properly.

Miss Duncan asks us if anyone knows anything about swallows. I put up my hand and tell her that every spring the swallows come back to our house and nest in the rafters of the barn. They lay eggs and hatch out their babies and fly in and out of the barn feeding them, but in the autumn they all fly away. Lots of other children in the class, particularly those who live on farms, tell the same story. Miss Duncan asks us if we know where the swallows go in winter. No one answers.

"They fly away to Africa where it is warmer," she says. "The swallows 'migrate' to Africa," and she writes the word, "migrate" on the

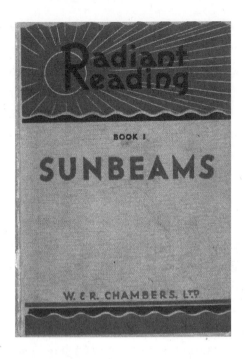

### 42. THE RULE OF THE CROSSING.

Two Fairies, three Pixies, four Elves and a Sprite
Came to the city at dead of night,
Walked upon pavements, pretending to be
Children of everyday people, you see.

158

They folded their shimmering wings, and tied
The tips with a ribbon at either side—
For everyday children can come and go
Only on everyday feet, you know.

The Fairies, the Pixies, the Elves and the Sprite
Had played for an hour in the silvery light,
When a Great Big Policeman spied them, and
crossed,
And bade them 'Good-evening,' and asked, 'Are
you lost?'

The Fairies, the Pixies, the Elves and the Sprite
Laughed, and said, 'No, we have come in the
night
To pretend to be everyday children, and play
Their everyday games in an everyday way!'

'Well, now,' said the Policeman, 'I'll teach you
a rule
That everyday children are learning at school.'
So they crowded round, listening, and learning
with pride
The Rule of the Crossing-from-side-to-side:

*Children, keep to the walls and hedges;*
*Children, stop at the pavement edges;*
*Look right, look left, and walk straight over;*
*For a road is a road, not a field of clover!*

159

"The Rule of the Crossing" by Isabel M Laird published in
Radiant Reading Book 1: Sunbeams

blackboard because it's a new word. The teacher shows us on a map where the swallows fly, over England, over France and Spain, over the sea to Africa and we are amazed that such small birds can fly such great distances. Derek Crichton asks how they know the way and the teacher says it's a bit of a mystery but they seem to be born with an instinct to guide them, and she writes the word, "instinct" on the blackboard because that's another new word.

Now it's time to read the story in the book. We take it in turns to read aloud, everyone in the class reading a sentence. Some children read easily, but others struggle. I always feel sorry for the slow readers. I keep my head down and don't stare but I can see them out of the corner of my eye, frowning at the page, pointing with their finger, stuttering and stammering as they try to make sense of the letters, feeling stupid and embarrassed, knowing everyone in the class is listening. It's often the big boys, the ones who are best at football in the playground, who are the slowest readers. The teacher is very patient, helping them to spell out the words they are finding difficult, sometimes asking them to read only a few words rather than a whole sentence. I expect she is thinking that, even if they find it difficult, they will only get better if they try.

Once we've read the story all the way to the end, the teacher asks us questions to make sure we've understood what we've been reading. We put our hands up and take turns at answering the questions.

"Which birds don't fly away in the winter? In the story, what do they say to try to persuade the swallow to stay? What happens which makes the swallow decide to go?"

We look at the drawings that go with the story and the teacher tells us that swallows have a patch of red at their neck, which we can't see because the drawing is in black-and-white, and asks us how we would recognise a swallow from its shape if it was flying overhead. I know the answer to that because I often watch them swooping over our courtyard with their forked tails and their curved wings. Miss Duncan says that, next time we have an Art lesson, we'll draw a picture of some swallows, but for now can we put away our Reading Books.

Next it's time to do some Writing. We lay our exercise book on the desk, open at a new page. The exercise book we use for Writing has lines to guide us so we know how far up to put the capital letters and how far down to put the tail of a "g" or a "p". I make sure my pencil is sharp and I lay out my rubber, ready in case I make any mistakes. When we started learning to write in Primary 1, we wrote on a slate with a slate pencil. I hated the scratchy, grating noise it made and having to use a wet sponge to rub out. I'm much happier with a pencil and a rubber. My brother, Stuart, who is in Primary 4, has started using pen and ink. Someone in the class has to go round all the desks every day filling up the inkwells and Stuart is always coming home with ink on his fingers and sometimes even on his shirt and trousers. Mum is not amused!

When we're all ready, Miss Duncan says,

"This morning, children, we're going to start learning how to do joined-up writing."

There's a murmur of excitement in the classroom. Joined-up writing is what grown-ups do. When Dad buys me a book, he writes my name, "Elizabeth," inside in his beautiful, slopey handwriting, and when Mum gives me a shopping list to take to Mrs Thompson's shop, she writes it in joined-up writing.

Miss Duncan draws lines on the blackboard, just like in our exercise books, then shows us how to write an "a", a "b" and a "c". We copy them into our exercise book making sure the loop of the "b" touches the top line. We practise writing a row of each letter separately and then we practise writing a row of "abc." At first my writing is slow and a bit wobbly, and there's lots of rubbing out, but each time I practise I get quicker and neater until I can do it easily.

Suddenly, the silent concentration in the classroom is broken by a "rat-a-tat" on the door. We look up and see the door open a fraction and the head of Mr Little, the Headmaster, appear.

"Excuse me, Miss Duncan, but have you heard the news?" he announces with great excitement. "There's a lion in the Manse Wood!"

I gasp with astonishment. A lion in the Manse Wood! How did it get there? Is there a circus in Aberdeen? Has the lion escaped from its cage? What if it eats the hens? What if it eats little sister, Sandra?

Mr Little smiles. "It's a dandelion," he announces, and goes out, closing the door behind him. We hear him chuckling to himself as he walks away along the corridor.

A dandelion! The other children laugh but I feel like a stupid fool. I am useless at knowing when people are joking. When someone tells me something, I always believe them. That's the trouble with being brought up in a family where we're taught never to lie, always tell the truth.

I should have known right away that Mr Little was joking. He likes teaching us words that have more than one meaning. Last week, he came wandering into the classroom, took off his bowler hat, stroked it and announced,

"I've never felt a felt like this felt felt."

Then he put his hat back on his head and went out the door.

After this latest interruption, it takes a minute or two for us to settle back to our writing practise. The teacher walks around the classroom making sure everyone is managing to form their letters correctly. After a while I hear her say,

"That's all we're going to do today. Well done. That's a very good start."

At twelve o'clock it's dinnertime. Children in the class, who come from Findon or Downies or from one of the farms far away from school, go to the Dining Room but we live nearby and so we can go home. I wait at the school gate for Stuart and Marilyn and we

Uncle Jim, Aunt Peg and cousins Newton, Pam, Bill, Ivan, Tommy
and Morris from Red Deer, Alberta, Canada

Aunt Nettie (Lenneta Phillips) from Echt

run home, hang up our coats at the back door and sit down at the kitchen table. Dad is there at the head of the table, with Sandra in her high chair next to him. He is sliding his hand round the back of her neck, tickling her cheek, then pulling his hand back quickly and looking away. Sandra is giggling and shouting,

"Daddy, stop tickling me."

Dad is looking surprised and pretending that it wasn't him. It's a game they often play. Mum takes a Shepherd's Pie out of the oven and starts dishing it up. Between mouthfuls, I tell everyone about the swallows and how they migrate in winter. I ask Dad if he knows where the swallows go when they leave in autumn.

"They fly away to Africa," he says. Dad knows everything. He has read lots of books.

Dad asks Marilyn what she has been doing at school this morning and she says she has been learning to count numbers up to twenty. So Dad asks her to count from one to twenty, then backwards from twenty to one and, when she does it without any mistakes, says, "Clever girl," and gives her a big smile. Our parents in different ways encourage us to work hard and do well at school. We're proud that our Dad is clever and has been to University and we want to please him and be like him. We also know that our Mum regrets her lack of schooling and is nervous and unsure whenever she has to write a report or make a speech at the Women's Guild. She is determined that we will have a good education and not miss out on opportunities as she did.

As we're eating our pudding, Mum asks Stuart what he has been learning at school today but he keeps his head down and mutters, "Nothing much." Stuart never likes to talk about school. He wolfs down his food as fast as he can, mumbles, "Please may I leave the table?" and before Mum has a chance to say, "No," is off, out the door, back to school to play football with his pals in the playground.

When Marilyn has finished eating, she helps Mum feed Sandra. I take Magnus, our little dog, for a run round the garden until Mum knocks on the kitchen window to tell me it's time to go back to school.

In the afternoon, Miss Duncan tells us we're having a Geography lesson. Hurrah! This is my favourite subject. I love finding out about the world. I love maps. Whenever I read a story in the Sunday School magazine about missionaries working in Africa or India or China, I get the big Atlas out of Dad's bookcase and find the places mentioned in the stories. I read out the names of the towns and cities, Bombay, Bangalore, Peking, Shanghai, Addis Ababa, Timbuktu, all so strange and exciting and far from Scotland. I wonder if I'll be a missionary when I grow up and go and work in these places.

Sometimes I turn to the page in the Atlas that shows the map of Canada because Mum has family living there. She told us that, when she was a little girl in Orkney, every Christmas a big box of apples used to arrive from an uncle who lived in British Columbia in Canada and what a treat it was because it was the only time she ever saw apples where she lived in Evie.

Mum has two brothers who emigrated to Canada. Her oldest brother, Bill, and his family live in Toronto, not far from Niagara Falls, and her brother, Jim, and his family live on a farm near Calgary. From time to time Mum gets letters from Aunt Maud and Aunt Peg. Her brothers don't seem to write letters but their wives do. Mum reads out the interesting bits and so we know that our cousins in Toronto have a summerhouse on Kashe Lake and go there for their holidays and pick blueberries on the lakeside to make blueberry muffins, and our cousins on the farm near Calgary go to school every day on horseback. Stuart steams the Canadian stamps off the envelopes and sticks them in his stamp album.

While I'm busy daydreaming about faraway places, Miss Duncan is pulling on a cord and down comes one of the maps that hang on rollers from the wall next to the blackboard. It's the map of Scotland, glossy and shining with pinks and lilacs and yellows to show the different counties and pale blue for the sea. The teacher picks up her long wooden pointer and says,

"Today, we're going to learn about the rivers in Scotland. Can anyone tell me the name of any of them?"

A forest of hands shoot up because we all know that we cross the bridge over the River Dee whenever we go to Aberdeen. Miss Duncan chooses someone to answer and then asks,

"What about the name of the other river that flows into the sea at Aberdeen?"

This is a bit more difficult but Sandy Milne puts his hand up and says that, when we go with the Sunday School for a picnic at Balmedie Beach, we cross the Bridge of Don.

Miss Duncan tells us there's a saying,

"The River Dee for fish and tree,

The River Don for horn and corn."

She asks if anyone has seen any fish in the River Dee. I put my hand up and tell her that sometimes we go for a run in the car up to Banchory and we stop at the Brig o' Feugh to watch the salmon jumping. I don't tell her that I feel really sorry for the fish because it looks impossible trying to swim upstream through torrents of brown, foaming water pouring through narrow crevices between the granite boulders. I listen to the thundering roar of the river and see the salmon leaping up, falling back, hurling themselves again and again against the rocks. I wonder if they ever get exhausted and just give up. I think I would.

Miss Duncan tells us that the salmon are driven by "instinct," just like the swallows in our reading book, to make their way up to the headwaters of the same river where they were born. There they will spawn and hatch out lots of baby salmon. I think about what the

Primary 4, Portlethen Primary School, 1953

Miss Jenkins with a group of Portlethen Primary School pupils on their way to the Aberdeen Festival of Speech and Drama, 1953

teacher is saying and begin to understand why the salmon keep trying to leap up the waterfalls. They are desperate to get home, just like I would be if I'd been away for a long time.

The teacher than asks if anyone has seen any trees near the River Dee. Linda McKay puts her hand up and says she's been on a visit to Balmoral Castle, where the King and Queen go for their holidays, and there were lots of trees all along the banks of the River Dee. Miss Duncan tells us that The Forestry Commission has planted acres of trees up Deeside, not sycamores or beeches or rowan trees that grow everywhere in Portlethen, but pine trees and spruce and larch, trees that will grow quickly, tall and straight, and be cut down and sawn up into planks for building houses and ships.

So now we understand why the saying is, "The River Dee for fish and tree," but what about, "The River Don for horn and corn?"

I remember once driving north of Aberdeen to visit Mum's brother, Sandy, who has a farm called "The Brae" near Keith and watching my cousins helping to harvest fields of corn, cutting and binding the grain, propping up the sheaves into stooks to dry in the sun and wind. I remember coming across the herd of black and white cows as they headed into the byre for milking and keeping a wary eye on their long, sharp horns. Does "horn and corn" just mean farming? But I don't know if Uncle Sandy's farm is near the River Don and so I don't put my hand up, but other children in the class do because they've got cousins who live on farms along the banks of the Don near Inverurie and Kemnay and Alford.

The teacher shows us the course of the rivers Dee and Don on her map, how they start in the hills as small burns, growing bigger and bigger as other streams join them, winding their way through their valleys till they reach the sea. She points to another river further south and tells us this is the River Tay, asking if anyone knows anything about the River Tay. Lots of hands go up because we all know the story of the "Tay Bridge Disaster", how, one stormy winter night, the bridge collapsed when a train was crossing, plunging the engine and all the passengers into the dark, deep waters below. Everyone was drowned. They say that, when you're crossing the new Tay Bridge in the train, you can look out the window and see the stumps of the old bridge still sticking out of the water. That would make me feel very nervous.

The next river Miss Duncan shows us on the map is the River Forth. Some children in the class say they have crossed over the Firth of Forth on the railway bridge when they were going on holiday to Edinburgh. I remember Dad driving us in his car onto the ferry at North Queensferry and the bumpety bump as we crossed the metal platform onto the deck of the ship. We were able to get out of the car and stand at the railing, watching as we passed the island of Inchgarvie with its pillboxes and gun emplacements still there from the War, listening to the rattle of the trains overhead on the Forth Bridge and the swish of water round the prow of the ship until we approached the pier at South Queensferry and had to get back into our car so we could drive down the metal ramp and along the road to Edinburgh.

The teacher points out the River Tweed on the map where they make the cloth with the same name, and the River Spey where they use the water to make whisky. She traces the course of the River Clyde and asks if anyone knows anything about this river. I'm able to tell the class that they build ships on the River Clyde and that the shipyards were bombed by the Germans in the war. Our Aunt Lena was a firewatcher in Paisley near Glasgow during the war and has told us very scary stories about hearing the sound of the German bombers flying overhead and then the whistle and the bang as the bombs exploded, lighting up the sky, setting fire to the shipyard workers' houses in Clydebank and Dumbarton.

Next, Miss Duncan asks Sandy Moir to get the atlases out of the cupboard and to pass them round the class. She gives us each a sheet of tracing paper and tells us to trace round the coastline of Scotland and, when we've done that, to trace the course of each of the rivers and write their names alongside them. We're to take the maps home and learn them because tomorrow we'll have a Geography test.

Now it's afternoon break time and we fetch our coats from the cloakroom and run out to the playground. I can see the janitor has been busy scattering sand over the frosty ground so they'll be no slides for the boys this afternoon. My friend, Kathleen, has brought her skipping rope with her and starts cawing the rope, jumping, chanting,

"I call in my very best friend
And that is Elizabeth."

I join her and we skip together counting,

"She's one, she's two, she's three, she's four," on and on till one of us trips and we stop. I step back and Kathleen starts skipping again but this time she calls in Mabel Tawse. I stand leaning against the wall and wait my turn to be called in again.

I look around the playground. I see a crowd of boys playing football and then I spot my brother, Stuart, doing some fancy footwork with a ball, kicking it up in the air, catching it on his boot, twirling round, hopping from one foot to the other. I think to myself, "Why is he showing off like that?" and then I realise he has an admiring audience. Two of the prettiest girls in his class, Cynthia McKay, Linda's big sister, and the new girl, Christian Rattray, with her big blue eyes and blond ringlets, are standing watching him. I know the girls like Stuart. They say they like his brown, curly hair and he's always chatty and friendly and smiling at them. I've heard lots of people say that he's charming. I know even Mum finds it hard to be cross with him. She has told us the story of how when he was little and being very naughty she said to him one day, "Stuart, what will I do with you?"

Pfaff sewing machine

Apparently, he gave her a big hug and said,

"Just love me, Mummy, " and that was the end of that telling off. And I've seen Mum chasing him round the garden, shouting,

"Stuart Dunn, just wait till I get my hands on you," but Stuart can outrun Mum and so he runs a bit, then turns round and laughs and calls,

"Come on, Mum. You can do it. Come and catch me."

Mum runs a bit more, trying to hold on to her crossness but soon she gives up and starts laughing, and that's the end of that telling off.

I wonder if I'm the only one who knows he's not always so

charming. Perhaps I should tell these silly girls how he pulls my pigtails just to annoy me and deliberately kicks his football at me, laughing when I scream at him to stop and have to dodge out of the way. I could tell them about how he tips the furniture out of my doll's house and uses it as a garage for his cars, and how he and Ralph Horne, the doctor's son, used me as a guinea pig to try out a raft they'd built, because I was smaller and lighter than them, and how I ended up soaking wet in the middle of a filthy, muddy pond when their raft sank. So he's not always charming. However, I have to admit that, very occasionally, when someone has been trying to push me around, it's been useful to be able to say,

"Stop that or I'll get my brother on you."

Just at that moment, the bell rings and we file back into the classroom. Miss Duncan reminds us that today is "Homecraft" day for the girls and so we leave the boys behind and troop across the playground to the room where Mrs Robertson, the Homecraft teacher, is waiting for us. We file in and find a chair behind one of the long tables and wait for the teacher to tell us what we will be doing.

Sometimes we knit, one row plain, one row purl, making long scarves or ties or belts. I remember learning to knit in Primary One with big needles and different coloured balls of wool, in, over, through, off, again and again till we'd finished the row, then swapping the needles into the other hand and knitting another row, until we'd formed a square. We had to take our knitting out to the teacher who examined it closely and, if she found any dropped stitches, she'd rip the whole thing out and we had to start again. Once she was satisfied that there were no mistakes, she'd cast off for us and throw our knitted squares into a box. She told us that she would sew all our squares together to form blankets that would be sent off to the soldiers who were still in Germany with the Army.

Mum knits almost every evening at home, sitting in front of the fire, listening to the radio. She knits all our cardigans and jumpers and can even knit socks on four needles, turning the heel, shaping the toes. She's been knitting since she was a little girl and is quick as lightning.

Today, however, we're not knitting. We're sewing. Last week the teacher gave us each a piece of red checked cloth cut into the shape of an apron and showed us how to tuck the frayed edges in by folding the material over and over again. We had to pin the hems, then tack them with big basting stitches. Now Mrs Robertson asks us to gather round her desk while she shows us how to do a slipstitch, taking little bites of the cloth at the back then a stitch into the hem, fixing it firmly into place. We go back to our tables and concentrate on sewing our hems carefully and neatly. The teacher walks round the class peering over our shoulders and, if she's not satisfied with anyone's work, they have to unpick it and start again.

I sit quietly sewing, thinking of how often I've watched Mum sewing a button back onto Dad's shirt, or mending a tear in Stuart's trousers. Sometimes she's darning a hole in one of my socks, weaving the big needle in and out between the strands of wool as if she was weaving a wicker basket. At other times, when she's making curtains or bedspreads or tablecloths, she lifts the cover off the sewing machine and we help her thread the cotton from the reel over lots of hooks and levers and through the eye the needle. For a long time, Mum was really worried about breaking a needle because the sewing machine is a Pfaff, made in Germany, and she couldn't get spare needles in this country. However, one day Dad came back from visiting the RAF station in Portlethen where he's the chaplain and said he'd been talking to one of the airmen's wives who was German and she said she might be able to help. A week or so later a parcel addressed to Mum arrived in the post from Germany and, when she opened it, there was a box of Pfaff sewing machine needles. Mum couldn't have been more pleased if she'd been given a box of diamonds. Now she can use the sewing machine with confidence and we watch her holding the material firmly, guiding it through from one side to the other, frowning with concentration, rocking her feet gently on the treadle to set the needle bobbing up and down. I often ask if I can have a go but she always says,

"No, not till you're older. You have to be very careful not to sew your fingers."

In the classroom, the teacher switches on the lights because in winter it starts getting dark quite early. We sit quietly concentrating on our sewing until Mrs Robertson tells us to finish what we're doing, hand in our work at her desk and go back to Miss Duncan. We cross the playground, holding on to each other in case we slip on the icy surface, and join the boys who tell us how they've been making tablemats out of raffia. I wonder why they don't teach the boys to sew? Perhaps they take it for granted that boys will always have a mother or a wife to sew on their buttons.

We take our seats and listen as Miss Duncan reminds us to be careful going home, particularly those in the class like Linda McKay who have to cross the main Aberdeen road. She tells us to remember the poem in our reading book,

"Children, keep to the walls and hedges.
Children, stop at the pavement edges.
Look right, look left, and walk straight over,
For a road is a road, not a field of clover!"

We empty the books out of our desks into our schoolbags, fasten the buckles, file out of the classroom, fetch our coats from the cloakroom, and make our way to the school gates. Then Kathleen, Sandy and I wait for Stuart and Marilyn and we walk home together at the end of another school day.

# February

Lena Dunn (Aunt Lena) with Sandra and Marilyn

# The Storyteller

Everyday life for us children in the Manse has just become much more interesting. Aunt Lena has come to spend a holiday with us. She's not actually our aunt, she's Dad's aunt, his father's youngest sister, but we never call her Great-Aunt Lena, just Aunt Lena. Most of the year, she lives in Paisley in a top floor flat that is full of dark mahogany furniture and glass-fronted bookcases. She is a member of a Book Club and gets sent a new novel in the post every month and so there are books everywhere. She teaches in a Primary School during the week and on Sunday she goes to church in Paisley Abbey. Aunt Lena is small, or at least smaller than Mum and Dad, and she has neat, dark, wavy hair that she covers with a hairnet when she's in bed at night. She has very small feet and wears shiny leather shoes with heels and straps and bows. She tells us that once, when she was younger, she went on holiday to France and was complimented on her "petite" feet. She says the word in French and we are very impressed. We've never even been to

England let alone France and we don't know any French words. She wears bright red lipstick and dusts her face with a big fluffy powder puff. We love when she comes to stay because she is interested in everything we do, talks to us all the time and is full of stories.

In the evening after tea we go through to the drawing room. Dad throws some more peat onto the fire, pulls the red velvet curtains shut, and switches on the lamp on top of the piano. Then he goes off to the kitchen to help Mum fill up hot water bottles to keep us all warm in bed at night. We gather round the fire. Aunt Lena sits in the armchair. Marilyn, Sandra and I cuddle up together on the couch. Stuart sprawls on the fireside rug, propping up his head on his hand.

"Tell us a story, Aunt Lena," we say. "Tell us a story about your school."

Aunt Lena thinks for a while then begins.


*Let me tell you about something that happened last week. It was Monday morning and the whole school was gathering in the hall for morning assembly. I felt a tug on my skirt and there was this child, Mary McGregor, holding out a pair of knitting needles and a ball of blue wool.*

*"Miss Dunn, I've dropped a stitch. Can you pick it up for me?"*

*"Mary," I said, "This is not the right time. You're a nuisance but give it to me. I'll fix it later."*

*The children were now filing into the hall. I had to go up on stage, and there I was with a bundle of knitting in my hand, not knowing what to do with it. I was walking past the piano and, on the spur of the moment, I lifted the hinged top of the piano and dropped the knitting inside out of sight. Assembly started with announcements, then the headmistress said that the school choir was going to sing, accompanied by Mrs Boorhill on the piano. Well, you can imagine Mrs Boorhill's surprise when the piano wouldn't play properly. She tried again, frowned, then stood up, opened the lid to investigate and discovered to her amazement a tangle of blue wool wrapped round the strings and the hammers!*

"Oh dear, Aunt Lena, did you own up?" we ask. "What did the Headmistress say? Did you get into trouble?" but Aunt Lena just laughs.

"Tell us another story," we say.

Aunt Lena thinks for a little while then starts speaking.

*Do you remember, Elizabeth, when you and Stuart came to spend a holiday with me - it would have been about the time Marilyn was born so you would have both been very young, about two or three? I was living in a bungalow then, with a garden, and for a little while after your Dad left to go home we were playing quite happily outside. But when we went in for tea, Elizabeth, you started crying and saying,*

"I want to go home. I want my Mummy."

"Are you sure, Elizabeth?" I said. You nodded your head.

"Well, just a moment. I'll need to phone the station master." So I lifted the receiver and dialled the number.

"Hello, Mr Station Master. I have a little girl here who would like to go home to Portlethen. Yes, I hear you. You want me to tie a label round her neck with her home address and bring her to the station. You say she can travel in the luggage van with the parcels and the guard. Thank you. I'll do that. Now where did I put my pen? Where's the labels?"

*Elizabeth, you were watching and listening and after a moment you said,*

"Aunt Lena, can I stay here with you? I don't want to go home in the luggage van."

"Good," I said, "because I need you and Stuart to help me paint the front gate."

*So we opened a pot of yellow paint and we painted the front gate and you both got paint all over your clothes but nobody cried and said they wanted to go home.*

Stuart looks up at me from his resting place on the rug in front of the fire and says,

"You silly idiot, Elizabeth. Fancy thinking Aunt Lena would send you home on your own in the luggage van among the suitcases."

"Well," I reply, indignantly, "I didn't know that. I was only little."

"Of course you were," says Aunt Lena. "Stuart's just teasing you."

It's dark outside now. We can hear the wind howling round the house and the old ash tree near the window creaking and groaning. Stuart prods the fire with the brass poker till the flames dance in the hearth and the smell of burning peat fills the room. Aunt Lena's face glows red in the firelight.

"Tell us a story about the War," says Stuart.

"Are you sure?" asks Aunt Lena, a bit anxiously.

"Yes, yes," we cry. "Tell us about the bombing."

Aunt Lena hesitates for a moment but then starts speaking.

*During the war, I was a fire-watcher in Paisley. After dark, I used to leave home and walk back to our school using a torch because there were no streetlights. I climbed up the stairs and out on to the flat roof of the school. It was my job to look out for any bombs falling and to let the Fire Service know where to go to put out fires and to rescue people. I also had to help the wardens make sure everyone obeyed the rules of the blackout - no one must show even a chink of light from their window because the German pilots could use the light to guide the bombs to their target.*

*One night I was sitting quietly, waiting, watching, when I heard in the distance the drone of aeroplane engines coming closer and closer. Wooo! Wooo! The sound grew louder and louder and I knew the German bombers were coming. I could hear them droning overhead, wave*

*after wave, moving north towards Clydebank with its shipbuilding
yards and its streets full of workers and their families. I listened as the
bombs began to fall. Whistle! Boom! Whistle! Boom! Boom! Boom!
I saw the flashes of light as one after the other the bombs exploded
until the sky to the north glowed red with the flames. I sat there on the
roof of the school and I could smell the smoke drifting on the night air
and I thought about the people of Clydebank in their battered homes,
blackout curtains flapping through shattered windows, streets filled
with debris and the scream of fire engines rushing to beat back the
flames.*

The four of us children sit in silence, eyes fixed on Aunt Lena's face
in the firelight, and we are there with her, hearing the bombs fall,
seeing the flames, smelling the smoke.

Just then, the drawing room door opens and in comes Mum.

"Time for bed, children," she says.

Reluctantly we get up, say good-night to Aunt Lena, leave the
drawing room and go to do all the things we usually do at bedtime
- drinking our cocoa, brushing our teeth, saying our prayers and
snuggling down in bed hugging the hot water bottle.

Sometime in the night I wake in panic. The bedroom curtains are
not properly closed - I am showing a chink of light. The bombers
can see the light and they are dropping their bombs on our house.
I am going to be killed, blown to bits. I must get out. I try to run
but my legs won't work. I can hear the whistle of the bomb falling.
It is coming to get me. I am terrified, shaking with fright, crying. I
climb out of bed, cross the landing to Mum and Dad's bedroom.
The moment the door opens, Mum lifts her head from the pillow as
if she was expecting me.

"Elizabeth, what's the matter?"

"The bombers are coming to get me. I didn't shut the curtains
properly. I'm showing a light," I sob.

"Sh. Sh, darling. You're dreaming. There are no bombers," whispers Mum. "Come here into bed beside me."

I squeeze into the bed and Mum wraps her arms around me, cuddling me against her warm body and at last I feel safe.

Next morning I overhear Mum saying to Dad,

"I'll be glad when Aunt Lena goes home and there's NO MORE STORIES."

# March

Sandra giving the hens some water to drink

# Counting our Chickens

We're out at the back gate waiting for the lorry to come. Marilyn and I are perched on top of the drystane dyke with little Sandra tugging at my skirt saying, "Help me up, Libby. I want to see too."

I pull her up and hold her close to keep her safe. Stuart has one foot on the bottom spar of the iron gate and we hear the creak of the metal hinge as he swings to and fro. We're all waiting, listening for the first sounds of an engine chugging up the Post Office brae, coming into sight round the corner of the Manse Road. We see clumps of yellow daffodils poking their heads through the tussocks of grass on the roadside and the first green leaves on the sycamore trees in the wood. There's a tractor harrowing in the field near Glascairn and a cloud of smoke puffing from a train on the railway line, but no sign of a lorry.

Every year at this time in the Spring, Mum orders a hundred day-old chicks from the supplier and this morning they are due to come.

We've been preparing for their arrival all week. We've chased away the cobwebs from the rafters of the outhouse and washed down the walls. We've swept the floor and covered it with a new layer of peat litter. We've carried the big square wooden brooder out into the fresh air and scrubbed it clean. We've shaken the dust out of the green felt, feather-filled bag that billows down from the lid of the brooder to make the little chickens think they're still snuggled under their mother hen. We've cleaned the wicks on the four round metal lamps, filled them with paraffin, covered them with lids and checked to see that they're working and giving out a gentle, even heat. We've poured fresh water into some of the troughs along the sides of the brooder and filled others with special chicken feed that smells just like the oatmeal we have in our porridge in the morning. Now the brooder is sitting in the centre of the outhouse, cosy and warm, waiting for the new arrivals.

We hear the slam of the kitchen door closing and see Mum march across the courtyard with a pail of pellets for the hens' breakfast. She fills up the feed dishes, and scatters some of the pellets on the ground.

"Hey, kittykittykitty," she calls and we watch the hens come running, out of the barn, round the corner from the drying green, down the courtyard, clucking and squawking, scratching and pecking as if they hadn't seen food for a week.

"Any sign of the lorry?" shouts Mum.

"No, not yet," Stuart answers.

We watch Mum open the door of the small outhouse next to the old byre and disappear inside. A minute later she comes back out and calls,

"Children, come and see this."

We can tell from her voice that she has something exciting to show us and so we hop down off our perches and run across the courtyard to join her.

"Sh," she says, "you must be very quiet."

She opens the door and we creep into the dimly-lit shed, closing the door behind us. Along the back wall is a wooden box filled with straw where a broody hen has been sitting on eggs for the last few weeks. Mum has been going in everyday to feed her but we'd almost forgotten she was there. We crouch down and peer into the nest and there, peeping out from under the hen, is a row of little heads, with sharp, pink beaks and bright dark eyes.

"They're baby turkeys," says Mum. "They've just hatched out."

"Can I hold one?" asks Marilyn.

Mum slides her hand slowly, carefully under the hen, lifts out a ball of fluff and hands it to Marilyn. The broody hen clucks softly but Mum talks to her soothingly and gives her some food to peck.

"Can I hold one too?" I ask.

Mum hands me a baby turkey, then one to Stuart and another to Sandra. I cradle mine in my hand, loving its grey-brown mottled coat and its shiny dark eyes. Sandra is rubbing her cheek against the soft down.

"Will it peck me when it gets big?" she whispers.

We all know why she's asking. Last year Mum bought six goose eggs, and hatched them out under a broody hen. They were very sweet when they were little but as they grew bigger they turned out to be a bit of a handful. Whenever someone came into the courtyard, they would gang up and run at them, necks stretched out, hissing and pecking. They frightened the paperboy so badly that he refused to deliver the Press and Journal to the back door. Me and Stuart and Marilyn soon learned to turn and face them, waving our arms and shouting, "Shoo, shoo," and they would back away, still hissing but not doing us any harm. Little Sandra wasn't able to stand up to them and often the geese would chase her round and round the courtyard till she ran screaming inside to Mum.

"No, darling," says Mum, stroking Sandra's hair. "They won't peck you. Turkeys are peaceful birds, not like geese. They'll say "Gobble gobble gobble," but they won't chase you."

"Good," says Sandra.

"Next time we come," says Mum we'll need to bring some food for the little ones. Do you know that little turkeys love dandelion leaves? Perhaps tomorrow you could gather some and we'll chop them up with their oatmeal."

Mum turns to look at the broody hen, murmuring,

"What a good little mother you are, sitting there so patiently. Now, can I see how your other eggs are doing?"

She slides her hand under the hen, lifting out a shiny, white egg, holding it in the palm of her hand. We look closely and see a hole in the shell and, through it, the wet, bedraggled feathers of a little bird starting to peck its way out into the world.

"Do you think we should give this one a helping hand?" asks Mum.

We nod our heads and watch as Mum carefully prises off a small flake of shell with her finger, making the hole just a little bigger.

"That should help. Right, back you go, little turkeys, and keep warm," says Mum, and pops all the baby birds back under the mother hen.

"Let's go and leave them in peace," she whispers and we tiptoe out, quietly closing the door behind us.

"Now, where's that lorry? It should be here by now," she says.

We return to our lookout posts at the back gate and wait. At last we hear the grunt and growl of an engine as it changes gear to climb the Post Office brae and the rattle and clatter as the lorry bounces over the ruts and puddles in the Manse Road. We run to tell Mum and watch as the lorry squeezes past the granite gateposts and into the courtyard. The driver jumps down from his cab, says hello to Mum, opens the back door of his truck and starts lifting out some small, square cardboard boxes. The air is filled with the sound of cheeping.

"Ten boxes, Mrs Dunn," says the lorry driver. "Ten chickens in each box. That's a hundred birds altogether. That's right, isn't it?"

"Are you sure they're Rhode Island Reds?" asks Mum. "We usually have White Leghorns but I thought we'd have a change this year."

"Good choice," says the lorry driver. "These Rhode Island Reds are grand layers and good for the pot as well."

I don't know if I want to think about our little chickens being "good for the pot," at least not today.

We watch the lorry driver climb back into his cab and drive out of the courtyard. We carry the boxes of chickens into the outhouse and shut the door.

"Right, now each of you take a box," says Mum. "Sandra, you come and share with me. Now lift the lid off carefully and count. We need to make sure there are ten chickens in each box."

I try to follow Mum's instructions but the chickens don't stand in rows and all these little cheeping bundles of fluff are very distracting.

"I've got eleven in my box," says Stuart.

"That's fine," says Mum. "I don't mind eleven, but what I don't want is nine. Now lift them out carefully one at a time and put them in the brooder."

I pick up a chicken and feel its little feet in my hands. I lay it gently on the floor of the brooder, then the next and the next, counting one, two, three, till I reach ten and the box is empty.

We count out the chickens in the other boxes and watch the brooder fill with a huddle of creamy-brown, cheeping balls of downy feathers.

"Now, lets put the lid back on," says Mum, and we each take a corner and set the lid down carefully, watching as the green felt bag falls gently onto the backs of the little birds.

"Come on," says Mum. "We'll leave them in peace to get used to their new home."

We don't really want to go and leave them but Mum says,

"Don't worry, we'll come back later and see how they're settling in. Now, let's go and have some dinner. Who wants egg and chips?"

I love egg and chips. I like dipping my chips in the soft, runny yolk. One of the good things about keeping hens is there's always plenty of eggs to eat: there's poached eggs for breakfast, scrambled eggs for tea, hard-boiled eggs with salad in summer, fried eggs with bacon on Sundays.

As I cross the courtyard, I watch the hens, plump as dumplings with their scarlet combs on top of their heads, pecking among the daisies and dandelions, scratching out hollows, fluffing their feathers, sending the dust flying into the air. It seems to me that our hens have a happy life. They get plenty of food to eat, clean water to drink and a comfortable perch in the barn to sleep on at night. They can roam all over the courtyard and drying green. They can fly over the wall into the wood and perch on the trees. They can crawl under the fence and scratch about among the grass in the field. The only place where they're not allowed to go is the garden because Dad gets very cross when they fly over the wall and scratch up his seedlings.

I remember the day when Sandra was the one watching out for intruders. She was still a baby and we'd been trying for weeks to coax her to talk but she wouldn't say anything. Then one day, when we were all in the kitchen eating our dinner, we heard this little voice coming from the high chair,

"Hen in the garden," and we all stared and clapped and were so excited about Sandra talking for the first time that we almost forgot to go and chase the hen off the garden wall.

After dinner, Stuart disappears on his bike up to Balquharn. He loves going to the farm. We're not quite sure what he does there except sometimes he comes home smelling strongly of silage and, one day, Mum got the shock of her life when she was passing by and saw him driving a tractor on his own in a field. I've heard her muttering that he should have been a farmer's son. Mum grew up on a farm and she's the only one of her sisters who did not marry a farmer.

Marilyn and I help Mum wash up the dishes then take Sandra out to the washhouse to play with the new kittens. A week ago we found our cats, Trixie and Mops, cuddled together in the tub of the boiler and, tumbling all over the two little mothers, a squirming bundle of newborn kittens. We counted and there were eleven altogether. Mum muttered something about having to find new homes for them but she said we could keep two for ourselves. So now we're sitting on the doorstep of the washhouse with some of the kittens on our laps trying to decide which of the eleven we want to keep. They're all so beautiful, tabby grey and white like their mothers, with coats that are soft as silk. I like the one that is mostly white with grey ears and clear blue eyes. Marilyn likes a dark one with a white nose and four white socks. Sandra loves them all and can't bear the thought of parting with any of them.

As I sit on the doorstep, stroking the kittens, I watch a blackbird gathering moss from the stones in the courtyard wall. Soon the swallows will be coming back for the summer, flying in and out of the top barn door, building their nests in the rafters. There are so many young animals and birds born in the Spring. I wonder why human beings are different, born higgledy-piggledy throughout the year? Dad and Stuart were born in Spring, in April, but Marilyn and I were Summer babies while Mum and Sandra were born in the middle of Winter. I must remember to ask Dad. He went to University so he's sure to know the answer.

In the evening, just before dark, Mum asks if we would like to go and see how the new chickens are settling into their new home.

"Remember to be very quiet so we don't frighten them," she says as we push open the door of the outhouse and go in. The air inside is warm with the smell of paraffin and full of the sound of cheeping. We crouch down on either side of the brooder and watch the little heads popping out through the wire mesh, pecking the meal, sipping the water.

"I'm going to pull out the tray and check that all the lamps are working," says Mum, "and I'll just tilt the lid open a tiny bit and see that everything's OK."

When Mum is satisfied that all is well, we tiptoe out saying,

"Goodnight, little chickens. Sleep well. See you in the morning," and leave, closing the door firmly behind us."

# April

Mrs Florence Dunn with Elizabeth, Marilyn and Sandra and cousins
Netta Wood and Agnes Stevenson at the front door of The Manse

# Spring Cleaning

**W**e can hear Mum singing as she comes up the stairs.
*"Lazy bones, sleeping in the sun,*
*How do you expect to get your day's work done?"*
Marilyn and I, snuggled down in our twin beds, look across at each other and smile. Mum often sings this song when she comes to wake us in the morning. She is still singing as she opens the bedroom door and comes in,
*"You'll never get your day's work done*
*Sleeping in the noonday sun."*
She stands for a moment by our bedside, smiling at us.

"Time to get up, girls. We've a busy day ahead of us. We're going to start the spring cleaning and I need you to help me."

Mum turns and walks briskly over to the window, flinging open the curtains. The sunshine streams in, bouncing off the wardrobe mirror, lighting up the dark corners of the room.

"Look," says Mum, "It's a lovely day, bright and breezy, just the kind of day we need to get the washing dried. Come along, up you get."

Mum leaves the room and goes back downstairs. We jump out of bed, dress as quickly as we can and run down to the kitchen. Stuart and little Sandra are there, eating their breakfast at the kitchen table. Dad is sitting in the armchair by the fire, lacing up his shoes. He's got on his old brown tweed trousers and his check shirt, so we know he is not going visiting round the parish this morning.

"I'll go and light the fire in the boiler for Mrs Moir," he says and disappears out the back door. Mrs Moir lives in Cookston Cottages and she comes on a Monday morning to help Mum with the cleaning. They usually start at the top of the house, working together as they move from room to room, chatting away as they dust and polish, but this is not going to be an ordinary cleaning day. We're going to be "spring cleaning."

Mum is bustling around the kitchen, throwing some peat on the fire in the range to heat the water, gathering dishes into the sink, making sure Sandra eats her breakfast, marshalling her troops.

"Stuart, can you tie a bit of clothes rope between the ash tree and the monkey-puzzle? We'll need it for the quilts and the carpets, and have a look in the cupboard under the stairs and see if you can find the carpet beater.

Elizabeth, Marilyn, as soon as you've had your breakfast, can you strip your beds and take the sheets and pillowcases out to the washhouse? Bring the blankets down to the bathroom and take the quilts out to Stuart in the front garden."

Marilyn and I finish our breakfast, carry our plates to the sink, and head for the stairs.

"Me come too," says little Sandra, trotting after us.

I look at Sandra and think, "You're probably going to be more of a hindrance than a help," but I can see she really wants to come with us, and I don't have the heart to disappoint her.

"Come on then," I say.

We go up to our bedroom and start pulling the quilts and the blankets off the beds. Sandra bounces on my bed, getting in my way.

"Sandra, you're a nuisance," I tell her, but she laughs and leaps across to bounce on Marilyn's bed. We pull the sheets from under her, tipping her off her feet, but she thinks it's great fun and gets up and bounces higher than ever. Marilyn and I strip the cotton pillowcases off the black and white striped pillows, throwing them onto the pile of bedclothes on the floor.

"Sandra, stop bouncing on that bed and come and help," I say. "You carry the pillowcases. We'll take the sheets. Now hold on to the banister and go downstairs one at a time."

I don't know how many times Mum has told me that it's my job to look after my little sisters when she's not there, and so I walk downstairs ahead of Sandra, making sure she doesn't trip and fall. We reach the foot of the stairs safely and make our way through the kitchen and out the back door. We can smell burning peat and look up to see smoke pouring out of the chimney above the washhouse. Dad has managed to get the fire going in the boiler. We step up onto the flagstone floor of the washhouse and there's Mrs Moir, not much taller than Stuart, round spectacles balanced on her nose, hair tied back in a bun, sleeves rolled up.

"Good girl, Marilyn. Drop the sheets in the basket. Elizabeth, let me take these from you. Well done, Sandra. What a big help you are."

We stand and watch as Mrs Moir fills a galvanised steel bucket from the tap in the corner of the washhouse and pours the cold water into the cast iron boiler. Dad is crouching down stoking the fire with bits of kindling and peat, blowing on it from time to time to keep the embers burning brightly. After a while he's satisfied the fire is well alight, and goes off to find out what else Mum needs him to do.

We stay and watch. Gradually we see the fire glow hotter and hotter and steam start to rise from the cauldron till it fills the whole of the washhouse. Mrs Moir lifts a packet of soap flakes from the windowsill and pours a handful into the hot water, stirring till it froths and hisses and bubbles. She picks up the white cotton sheets and plunges them into the wash, stirring and poking, lifting and turning with a long wooden stick.

"Stay well back, girls. This is very hot," she says. She turns to lift up the bucket, fill it with water from the tap, and empty it into one of the two wooden tubs along the back wall, ready for rinsing.

Just then, Mum appears in the washhouse.

"How're we doing, Mrs Moir?" she asks. She peers through the steam at the sheets bubbling in the boiler, then turns to smile at us.

"Come on, girls. I need your help inside," she says. We leave reluctantly and follow her back into the house.

"Can you fetch the blankets?" she says.

We carry the blankets in our arms downstairs and into the bathroom. Mum has already filled the bath with warm, soapy water. She takes the blankets from us and drops them in. Now we're happy and excited because we know what comes next.

"Off with your shoes and socks. Tuck up your skirts and in you go," says Mum. Marilyn and I climb in and Mum lifts little Sandra and sets her down in the water. And then we tramp, tramp, tramp, up and down, squeezing, squelching, holding hands and jumping, splashing the water till Mum squeals in protest,

"Right, girls, that's enough. Out you come."

"Just a little bit longer," we plead because this is good fun. We stamp our feet, squashing and squishing, shouting and laughing until, eventually, we can't protest any longer and have to come out. We dry our feet and legs on a towel, put our socks and shoes back on. Mum is fishing the blankets out of the bath.

"Elizabeth," she says, "Take an end. I'll turn the blanket this way.

You turn it in the opposite direction so we squeeze some of the water out. Good. Now put it in the basket. Marilyn, do you want to do this one with me?"

So Marilyn takes hold of an end and twists and turns until all the blankets are squeezed and packed in the wicker basket. I take one handle, Marilyn the other and we carry it through the kitchen, leaving a trail of dripping water, and out to the washhouse. Mrs Moir picks up the blankets and plunges them into the cold clear water in the sink, swirls them around, then lifts them into the second tub for a final rinse.

"Mrs Moir, can I turn the handle on the mangle?" I ask.

"Yes," she answers, "but you must keep your fingers away from the rollers."

She lifts the blanket out of the sink, folds it in half lengthways, then again till it is just the right size.

"Right, Elizabeth, turn the handle slowly."

I crank the handle and watch as Mrs Moir carefully feeds the end of the blanket in between the rollers and the water streams out into a bucket. Marilyn catches the blanket at the other side and dumps it in the basket. Now it's Marilyn's turn to crank the handle and I catch the next blanket and let it fall into the basket. Mrs Moir turns the wheel on the top of the mangle to tighten the rollers and we feed the blankets through the mangle to give them a second squeeze. When all the blankets are rinsed and mangled, we carry the basket across the courtyard, past the hens scratching and pecking among the dust, round the corner of the outhouses to the back drying green. Mum is there, pegging out the sheets, with Sandra holding the basket of pegs, handing them up to Mum one at a time.

"Well done, girls," says Mum as we set the basket down on the grass. "Look at that lovely wind. The washing will dry in no time."

We can feel the wind blowing strongly from the west, down

Stuart, a visitor, Elizabeth, Marilyn, Rev Alexander Dunn and friends from Glasgow University in the drying green at the Manse, with a view over The Glebe and the Findon Burn towards Hillside.

Magnus, our Shetland collie

from the hills behind Cairnwell, over the waving grass, through pink clover and golden buttercups in the fields below Balquharn, buffeting the white cotton sheets flapping on the line. Marilyn runs and hides behind one of them.

"You can't see me," she shouts.

"Yes, I can. I can see your feet," I answer. We chase each other round and round the clothes poles, in and out among the wet sheets till Mum tuts that we'll be putting dirty marks on her nice clean washing.

"Off you go and see if your Dad and Stuart need help with the carpet. Sandra, you stay with me. I need you to pass me the pegs."

We find Dad and Stuart in our bedroom getting ready to lift the carpet.

"Stuart," says Dad, "When I take the weight of the bed, pull the carpet out from under it. Ready, one, two, three, pull."

Dad lifts the foot of my bed and Stuart pulls the carpet, sliding it over the linoleum surround. Dad lifts the foot of Marilyn's bed and Stuart pulls till the carpet lies in a heap in the middle of the floor.

"We need to roll it up and carry it downstairs," says Dad. "Elizabeth, Marilyn, come and help."

We get down on our hands and knees, take hold of the tasselled fringe and roll the carpet till it looks like the picture in the story of Ali Baba and the Forty Thieves. We lift it, tuck it under our arms and manoeuvre it carefully out the bedroom door, down the stairs, through the hall and out the front door. We heave the carpet over the rope stretched between the ash tree in the corner of the garden and the monkey-puzzle in the middle of the lawn. Stuart grabs the cane handle of the carpet beater and whacks with all his strength, sending a cloud of dust into the air. Whack, whack, whack he goes along one side, thump, thump, thump along the other.

"Can I have a go?" I ask.

Stuart hands me the beater and I whack as hard as I can. The dust tickles my nose, making me sneeze, but it's good fun being able to hit something with all my might and not get into trouble. After a while I hand the beater to Marilyn and she thumps the quilts, stirring the feathers till they fluff and flutter inside their Paisley-patterned covers.

We hear Mum calling, "Dinner Time", and we throw down the carpet beater, run inside, wash our hands at the kitchen sink and sit down at the table. Dad is there in his usual place at the top of the table, but now he's dressed in the suit and tie he wears when he's going out visiting round the parish. Mrs Moir comes and joins us and we all share a big Shepherd's Pie, full of mince from the butcher and carrots and potatoes from the garden.

After lunch, Mum goes to the door to bid Cheerio to Mrs Moir, saying "Thank You," and "See you next Monday." Dad fetches his coat and scarf from the hall, leaves by the back door, and we hear him reversing his car out of the garage, turning around in the courtyard and driving off down the Manse Road.

"Right," says Mum, "There's still a lot to do but first we need to clear up. I'll wash the dishes. Elizabeth, you dry and Marilyn, you put away. Stuart, you're in charge of Sandra."

In the afternoon, we go back up to our bedroom. Mum stands on a chair to unfasten the brass hooks and take down the velvet winter curtains, replacing them with light, cotton curtains with a border of pink and blue flowers. She washes the window, then leaves it open to air the pillows draped along the window ledge. She mops the lino floor and washes the tiled fireplace and I remember cold frosty nights, when Dad lights the fire in our bedroom, and we lie in bed watching the firelight dance and flicker on the ceiling.

Marilyn is busy chasing away the cobwebs with a long handled feather duster. Sometimes she swipes a bit too energetically, shaking loose one of the feathers, catching it as it flutters down. I polish the oak chest of drawers and the wardrobe with Mansion polish till the air is filled with the scent of beeswax. We huff and puff as we help Mum turn the mattresses till the up becomes the down and the top becomes the bottom.

At last when the room is clean and shining with not a speck of dust, Mum stands, hands on her hips, and says, as she often does,

"Cleanliness is next to godliness. If we can't be godly, we can at least be clean."

She gathers up all the mops and dusters and turns to leave the bedroom.

"Right, girls. Let's go and fetch the carpet."

We follow Mum down the stairs, through the hall and out the front door. What a surprise! Little Sandra has persuaded Stuart to help her turn the carpet into a tent. He's loosened the rope till it sags, pulled the fringes of the carpet out and weighed them down with stones from the rockery. He's spread a tartan rug for her and she's sitting happily inside the tent with Magnus, our Shetland collie, at one side and Mokey, her furry toy donkey at the other.

"Sandra darling," says Mum, "We need to take the carpet back upstairs."

Sandra's head drops onto her knees, her soft, silky hair hiding her face, the picture of disappointment. Mum watches her for a moment.

"I'll tell you what," she says, "Let's all have a break for afternoon tea since we've been working so hard."

She turns and disappears in through the front door.

"Sandra," I say, "Can me and Marilyn come into your tent?"

Our little sister looks happy again and moves over so that we can crawl inside. There is a lovely, musty smell just like old potato sacks, and it feels warm and cosy, sheltered from the wind. We tell Sandra that we really like her tent. Magnus likes it too because his tail is wagging. We pat and stroke him and try to stop him licking our faces.

Soon Mum comes out carrying a tray, spread with an embroidered tray cloth, and on it a teapot, milk jug and sugar bowl, some china teacups and saucers and a plate of shortbread biscuits. Stuart fetches a chair and Mum sits down and pours out the tea. We sit together, drinking cups of warm sweet milky tea, crunching the shortbread biscuits, smuggling a few broken bits to Magnus. We listen to the wind rustling the leaves and the sparrows chirping in the beech hedge behind us, and watch the clumps of daffodils bordering the gravel path sway in the breeze.

When we've finished, Mum gathers the cups and saucers on to the tray, saying,

"Sandra, will you come with me to see if the washing's dry. I need you to hold the peg bag for me. Magnus, you can come too."

Sandra crawls out of the tent, holding on to the little dog and the two of them follow Mum into the house.

Stuart starts to dismantle the tent, carrying the stones back to the rockery, tugging the carpet off the washing line. We help him roll it up like a sausage and manoeuvre it back up the stairs and into our bedroom. Stuart and I between us manage to lift the foot of the bed and Marilyn crawls underneath, rolling the carpet back into place.

Just as we finish, we hear the back door opening and run down to the kitchen to tell Mum we've laid the carpet.

"Goodness me! Well done! How did you manage that? These beds are heavy," says Mum, setting down the wicker wash basket, brimming with clean sheets and blankets, on the kitchen table.

"Stuart, can you fetch the clothes horse," says Mum, "And set it up by the fire. We need to get the washing aired before it can go back on the beds. Elizabeth, Marilyn, can you each take a corner of this sheet. Give it a good tug to smooth out the wrinkles. Now fold it in two and hang it over the clothes horse."

We smooth and fold and drape the sheets and blankets and hang them where the warmth from the fire in the range can dry out the last drops of moisture.

We hear Dad's car drive into the courtyard and run to the back door to welcome him home.

"How's the Spring Cleaning going?" he asks. "Have you managed to get the washing dry?"

He hangs his overcoat and scarf in the hall, sits down on a kitchen chair to take off his shoes.

"Where's my slippers?" he asks, "And where's Sandra?"

We look around the kitchen in surprise. Sandra has disappeared.

"I'm here," says a little voice. Sandra has managed to crawl through the bars of the clotheshorse and has made herself a new tent under the blankets, and there she is, sitting happily on the fireside rug with her arm round Magnus.

After tea, we carry the clean sheets and blankets upstairs to our bedroom and Mum shows us how to tuck in the bottom sheet securely with "hospital corners," the way she learned when she was nursing in Glasgow. We shake the pillows back into their pillow-cases and spread the feather filled quilts, plump with fresh air, back on top of the blankets.

At bedtime, when Mum comes to tuck us in and hear our prayers, she says,

"You've been such a help today," and gives us a big hug.

We snuggle down in our warm, clean beds and breathe in the scent of the wind blowing down from the hills through fields of buttercups till we fall asleep.

# May

Mrs Florence Dunn presenting a prize to
Marilyn Dunn at Portlethen Primary School

# Hens, Swallows & Amazons

We're home from school and Marilyn and I run upstairs, dump our schoolbags, wriggle out of our school uniform and into dungarees and old jumpers. We clatter downstairs to the kitchen where Mum is busy preparing vegetable pie for tea, standing at the sink in her flowery apron, peeling potatoes, chopping up carrots and turnips. We can smell onions frying in the pot on the cooker and hear the crackle of peat burning in the range. Mum looks up and smiles.

"The egg basket is on the table, girls. Be careful," she says.

It's our job to collect the eggs when we come home from school and Mum is always telling us to be careful. Does she mean, "Be careful when you're climbing the ladder up to the nest boxes or balancing on the open rafters above the garage?" I don't think so. We are children who climb to the top of the tallest trees in the Manse wood, play in the fast-flowing burn, scramble around the rocks and cliffs at the shore, leap over the ditches and the deep, dark pools of peaty water in the Moss. If Mum were to be worrying every time we did anything dangerous, she'd be a nervous wreck. No, what she means is to be careful and not crack any of the eggs because then they can't be sold to the Egg Marketing Board when the lorry comes to collect the trays on Thursdays. We know it's the egg money that pays for our music lessons and party dresses and holidays, and so we're always careful.

We pick up the basket, go through the scullery and out the back door. Little Sandra is playing on the doorstep with Trixie, our cat, wrapping her in a blanket and cuddling her down in her doll's pram. We stop to admire her furry, whiskered "baby" before skipping out through the garden gate and into the courtyard. There's no sign of Stuart: he's off somewhere on his bike as usual, and the garage doors are standing open so Dad's away as well, probably visiting the Royal Infirmary in Aberdeen. Dad's the minister and visits everyone from Portlethen when they go into hospital. I've heard Mum tutting crossly, saying that he likes going hospital visiting because there are lots of pretty young nurses on the wards who make a fuss of him. Dad says nothing, just drives off into town with a twinkly smile and a wave of a hand out the car window.

We stop for a minute in the courtyard to look up at the swallows, perched on the telephone lines, wheeling over the outhouses, skimming the rooftops, swooping down and in through the barn door. I love the noise they make, the squeaks and squeals of excitement, like friends chatting to each other. Dad tells us how our swallows fly north from Africa every year, over the Sahara, along the coast of Portugal and Spain and France, across the Channel to England. They don't stop in London or York or Edinburgh but fly on till they see the very best place to spend the summer, and that's The Manse at Portlethen. It's two or three weeks now since our swallows came back and we've been watching them build their nests in the rafters and eaves of the barn, snuggling down to lay their eggs in the dusty, cobwebby corners high above the hens, clucking and scratching in the peat litter on the floor below.

Marilyn tugs my sleeve to remind me we've work to do. We start in the washhouse with its wooden tubs and cast iron boiler. We climb the dusty, creaky steps to the loft and clamber gingerly over the rafters to the nest under the eaves above the garage. The hens have warm, straw filled nest boxes in the barn but the silly things choose all sorts of nooks and crannies to lay their eggs. Sure enough, there's a hen sitting on top of the wall. Marilyn crouches down and holds out her hand. Is it a pecker? The hen fixes her with a round pink eye and jabs at her with its beak. Marilyn pulls the sleeve of her jumper down to cover her fingers and, bravely ignoring the pecks, slips her hand under the hen and brings out three lovely warm brown eggs for me to put in the basket. The hen clucks crossly but stays sitting on her nest.

We make our way carefully back over the rafters, down the wooden stair and out into the courtyard. We go next door to the old stable, stacked high with peat for the fires in winter, full of the scents of dried, dusty, twiggy heather and gorse that grow in Portlethen Moss in summer. I climb the stack, using the blocks of peat as steps, reach my hand along the top of the wall and find two more eggs for the basket.

We leave the stable, turn right and go into the barn, peering through the shadows until our eyes get used to the darkness, wrinkling up our noses at the sharp smell of ammonia mixed with peat litter. During the day, most of the hens are outside in the courtyard but there are always a few in the barn, sitting quietly and contentedly on the perches. Today something is different. The hens are up on their feet, pacing to and fro, squawking noisily.

"What's wrong with you?" I ask them. "Is there a cat about?"

"Perhaps there's a rat," whispers Marilyn.

Ugh! I hate rats, with their small beady eyes and long, thin grey tails, skulking along the walls, disappearing into dark holes under the foundations. I hand the basket to Marilyn and start to climb the ladder to the nest boxes. Suddenly, I realise we are not the only people in the barn. Above my head in the shadows I hear a whispering and a scraping of feet and a creaking in the rafters. I look up and gasp with shock because there, looking down at me, are three boys, not boys from my class at school, not friends of my brother, but big lads from the Secondary School. They are standing on the rafters, holding on to the roof beams, rifling through the swallows' nests. I rattle down the ladder, grab Marilyn's hand and pull her behind me out of the barn. We run helter-skelter across the courtyard and into the kitchen screaming,

"Mum, Mum, there's boys in the barn and they're stealing the swallows' eggs."

I see Mum frown and purse her mouth in the way she does when she's not pleased about something. She wipes her hands on the dishtowel, stomps out of the kitchen, across the courtyard and into the barn. Marilyn, Sandra and I trail anxiously after her.

"Come down out of there this instance," Mum rages. "How dare you! Get out of here!"

We see Mum standing just inside the barn door, dressed in her flowery apron and furry slippers, feet planted firmly, hands on her hips, still clutching the dishtowel. We hear mutterings and shuffling of feet and then a thump as one boy drops down onto the floor of the barn. He's a big sturdy lad, bigger than Mum, but he cowers as he tries to sneak past her.

"Get down that road and don't let me see your face again," says Mum and out flashes an arm and thwack goes the dishtowel round the back of the lad's head. We watch wide-eyed as he runs past us, across the courtyard, out the back gate and disappears down the Manse Road.

We hear a thump of feet, then another as the second and third lads drop down from the rafters, a whack from Mum's dishtowel, a yelp of hurt and humiliation, a thundering of boots across the courtyard as they flee. Three hefty country lads are no match for our Mum, armed with her dishtowel and the wrath of God.

I hear Mum mutter, "The cheek of them," as she marches back across the courtyard, slams the kitchen door and goes back to her potato peeling. We watch her go, proud that nothing frightens our Mum. Thanks to her the swallows' eggs are safe. Mum has saved the day.

# June

Marilyn, Sandra, Marylen Hourston (cousin), a visitor,
and Elizabeth, along with Magnus, the Shetland Collie,
and Trixie and Mops, the kittens

# Running Away from Home

"It's not fair. I can't do anything right," I mutter to myself. "I've had enough. I'm running away from home."

I stomp into the hall, grab my coat, flounce through the kitchen and out the back door. My little sister, Sandra, is playing with her doll on the doorstep. She looks up.

"Libby, where are you going?" she asks.

"I'm running away from home and never coming back," I declare.

I march along the path, through the gate into the courtyard. I pass the washhouse and there's Mrs Moir, our cleaning lady, sleeves rolled up, bending over the steaming hot tub, pummelling some clothes on the wooden scrubbing board. I usually go and help her to crank the handle of the mangle, but not today. I stride across the courtyard, scattering the hens with a squawk and a flutter.

"Out of my way, hens," I shout, waving my arms as I march on.

"Libby, wait for me," calls a little voice behind me.

I glance over my shoulder. Oh no, it's Sandra, in her flowery summer dress, yellow ribbon bobbing in her hair, trotting after me on her short little legs.

"Go away. I'm running away from home and I'm never coming back," I say again.

"I'm coming with you," says Sandra with determination.

"No you're not. Go back to Mummy," I order.

I march on, across the courtyard, round past the hen house, through the drying green, ducking under the newly washed sheets and towels flapping in the wind.

"Libby, wait for me," cries a pleading little voice. I look back. Sandra is running as fast as her legs will carry her, tripping, falling, picking herself up.

"Sandra, go back," I say angrily.

"No. I'm coming with you," Sandra insists.

I squeeze through the wire fence, and set off across the field. Behind me I hear puffing and panting. I stop and look back. My little sister's still there, stumbling through the long grass, doggedly, determinedly following me.

"Wait for me, Libby," she cries again.

I huff with exasperation, but I give up and wait for her.

"You're a nuisance," I tell her, but she just smiles at me as I take her hand. She skips happily along beside me as we dodge the thistles, heading up the hill, following the burn. At the top of the field we reach the drystane dyke that marks the end of the Glebe. We can go no further. I find a flat rock overlooking the muddy hollow where the cows come to drink in the burn and we sit down side by side. Sandra wriggles and fidgets, trying to find a comfortable seat on the knobbly, granite boulder, drumming her heels on the mosses and lichens that cling to the rough stone. After a minute or two, she jumps down and wanders off to explore. I look back across the field to the big stone house where we live and see the window of Mum and Dad's bedroom staring back at me. I expect Mum's there at this moment, making the bed, dusting the dressing table, gathering up clothes for Mrs Moir to wash. I wonder if she's missing me yet and feeling sorry she was so cross with me this morning.

Sandra comes back with a fistful of wild flowers. She hands me a daisy and watches as I pull the petals off one by one.

"He loves me. He loves me not," I count. "He loves me. He loves me not. He loves me."

"Hooray," laughs Sandra, clapping her hands.

She hands me a buttercup and tilts her chin up.

"Do you like butter?" I ask, holding the buttercup under her chin. "Let me see. Yes, your chin is yellow so you really like butter."

Sandra smiles and drops the rest of her posy in my lap.

"Libby, will you make me a daisy chain?" she asks and I carefully use my thumbs to split the stems then thread the little flowers together till I've joined them all in a circle. I set the daisy chain carefully on her soft brown hair and think to myself that my little sister can be a nuisance at times but she is also very sweet and as pretty as a picture. I lift her up to sit beside me and we watch the brown, peaty water splashing over the boulders in the burn and listen to the cows in the next field, swishing through the long grass, mooing softly as they graze.

After a minute or two I hear a pleading little voice.

"Libby, I'm cold. I want to go home."

"I'm never going home," I remind her. "I'm running away."

The sun is shining but there is a chilly wind blowing in from the sea. I take off my coat and wrap it round Sandra's shoulders, put my arm around her and hold her close. I can feel her shivering. We sit a little while longer. Sandra starts to cry, big tears rolling down her cheeks.

"I want to go home," she sobs.

I look down at her tearful face, and her bare legs dangling from the cold, hard rock and give up.

"Come on then. We'll go home," I say.

Sandra stops crying and wipes her tears on the sleeve of her cardigan. I take her hand and we walk slowly down the hill, through the field, heading home. We squeeze through the fence, cross the drying green into the courtyard, make our way past the hens scratching and pecking among the grass and the gravel, push the back door open and go into the house. Mum is in the kitchen, sitting at the table, chatting and having a cup of tea with Mrs Moir. She looks up and smiles.

"Hello, darlings. You're just in time. Dinner's nearly ready."

What a disappointment! I realize with dismay that I've run away from home, been gone for ages and Mum has never even noticed!

# July

Rev Alexander Dunn, Elizabeth, Stuart, Marilyn and Sandra Dunn with
Eric, Joy, and Christine Pearson at the funfair at Aberdeen beach.

# The Shetlanders

## Arrival

It's early in the morning and we're standing on the quayside at Aberdeen harbour looking up at the dark steel hull of the St Clair, wisps of steam and smoke still drifting out of the funnel after its overnight sailing from Shetland. Everywhere is bustle and activity. We gaze up at the ship's cranes swinging overhead, lifting boxes and packing cases out of the hold and dumping them on the quay. We watch the queue of passengers heaving suitcases down the gangway, and porters with luggage trolleys weaving to and fro among lorries and taxis. We scan the crowds of people and then we spot them, a row of little blond heads peering over the wooden rail on the top deck, shouting, waving excitedly. It's the Pearson family. There's Eric with Joy and Christine next to him. Behind them is Aunt Jemima with little Ronald in her arms. We wave back to let them know we've seen them.

R.M.S. St. Clair                                    P. Sinclair

"Where's Uncle Sandy?" asks Stuart.

"He'll be waiting for his car to be off-loaded," says Dad.

Every year in July, the Pearson family come south to spend a holiday with us at Portlethen. Sandy and Jemima Pearson have been friends with Mum and Dad since before we were born. I once asked Mum how they'd all met and she told me the story. Dad had just left Glasgow University and was working as a minister in Northmavine in the north of Shetland. He met Jemima Halcrow, the teacher in nearby North Roe Primary School, and when Jemima heard that the new district nurse was arriving on the overnight boat from Aberdeen, she suggested that Dad went to Lerwick to welcome her. Mum said she was struggling down the gangway with a heavy suitcase and saw this young man standing on the quay, smiling at her and was annoyed that he wasn't offering to help. This was not a good start to their relationship, but, by the time Dad had driven her to her lodgings in Ollaberry, he had so impressed her with his charm that it wasn't long before they were going out together as a couple. Mum said Dad was very kind and used to come with her when she was called out as the midwife, even in the middle of the night. She said he would stay downstairs, reassuring the new father, while she was upstairs helping the mother to give birth.

Mum also got to know Jemima and, when the teacher from North Roe married a colleague called Sandy Pearson, all four young people became friends, and have stayed in touch throughout all the years. Sandy Pearson is now the Headmaster at the school in Walls, which they pronounce "Waas," and they all live in the Happyhansel Schoolhouse, close to the seashore in the west of Shetland. Every summer during the school holidays they sail from Lerwick to Aberdeen and we go to meet them off the ship.

So now we're standing on the quayside in the early morning sunshine waiting for the Pearsons to disembark. As we watch, Uncle Sandy appears on deck, hovering anxiously as their green Standard 8 car is lifted out of the hold in a sling hanging from a crane, swung over the side of the ship and gently lowered on to the quay. We can almost hear his sigh of relief as the wheels touch the ground. Then he gathers his family and leads them down the gangway and over to where we're standing, holding out his arms to hug us, shaking Dad's hand, patting him on the back. Aunt Jemima gives us all a hug, saying how we've grown since last year. After a few minutes of welcoming chat, Dad points out where his car is parked and Uncle Sandy and Aunt Jemima bundle their family into their car and follow Dad's little black Singer as we bump our way over the granite setts, out of the harbour, across the River Dee, up the hill and along the road towards Portlethen.

At one point I turn to make sure they're following us and am amazed to see that it's Aunt Jemima who is driving. What a surprise! We never see our Mum driving even though we know she passed her driving test and had a car of her own when she worked as a district nurse in Shetland.

"Why is Aunt Jemima driving?" I ask Dad.

"Your Aunt Jemima has been driving for a long time, even before she met Uncle Sandy. In fact, she taught Uncle Sandy to drive."

Well, this is interesting. It's always the men who drive the cars in

Portlethen, and the tractors, and the delivery vans. Perhaps they do things differently in Shetland.

Soon we reach Portlethen, turn down at the crossroads, then up the Manse Road. As we swing through the back gate into the courtyard, Magnus, our little Shetland collie, runs to meet us, jumping up and down, tail wagging furiously, barking with excitement, bringing Mum hurrying out of the house to hug and kiss the visitors and bid them welcome.

"Come away in," says Mum, "How was the journey? You must be hungry. Have you had any breakfast?"

"The steward brought us a cup of tea and a cream cracker," says Christine.

"Well, that's not enough for growing bairns," says Mum. "Come away in and I'll make you some poached eggs and toast."

Suddenly, the kitchen is full of Shetland voices, lilting and singing like music. We're so used to Mum's Orkney accent that we hardly notice it but the Shetlanders sound different. I know from History lessons at school that they were speaking Norwegian until a few centuries ago and I expect that's why they sometimes use words, or have ways of pronouncing words, that are different.

"How's the peerie lass?" asks Aunt Jemima, giving Sandra a hug. The Shetlanders say "peerie" instead of "little" and "du" instead "you" and "ting" instead of "thing." It sounds strange at first but I rather like it.

Mum is doing what she always does to make people feel welcome. She is feeding them as much as they can eat, everything fresh and homemade, with lots of encouragement to eat just a little bit more. Eventually she is satisfied that no one will starve and says,

"Right, children, off you go and play in the garden," and we know that she wants peace to talk to Aunt Jemima and catch up with family news.

# The Garden

The Manse with its courtyard and walled garden

We jump up from the kitchen table, and go out the back door into the courtyard. Stuart takes Eric to see his new bike and we take Joy and Christine for a look at the hens and chickens. They want to start collecting eggs but we tell them that it isn't time, but we'll do it later. We go through the gate into the garden with its high walls covered in fruit bushes, and its orderly rows of potatoes and carrots and lettuce, full of the scent of roses and sweet peas and marigolds.

"Can I pick a raspberry?" asks Joy.

"Of course," I say, "Pick as many as you like. Don't you have raspberries at home?"

"No," says Joy. "We do have strawberries and gooseberries but they're much smaller than yours and they're not ripe yet."

"Can I pick this strawberry?" asks Christine. "It's enormous."

I realise that they don't have a garden full of plump, ripe black-currants, and raspberries, gooseberries and strawberries. We take it for granted that we can pick fruit straight from the bush throughout the summer but for them it is a treat.

We wander along the paths and I see Joy and Christine looking up at the sycamore trees over the wall in the wood. I know from pictures that Shetland has almost no trees because it is so windy and realise that our very ordinary sycamores are as exotic to them as palm trees would be to us.

"Would you like a swing?" asks Marilyn.

Joy and Christine nod their heads and we skip down the gravel path to the big beech tree in the middle of the front lawn. A few years ago, Dad climbed up and tied two ropes from a branch and drilled holes in a plank of wood to make a seat for our swing.

"Don't you have a swing at home?" asks Marilyn,

"Yes," says Joy, "But it's much smaller than this."

We let Joy go first and she perches rather nervously, clutching the ropes. Marilyn gives her a gentle push, then another, giving her time to find her confidence. Gradually we can see her start to smile and enjoy herself.

"Do you want to go higher?" asks Marilyn.

Joy hesitates, then screws up her eyes and nods her head, and soon she's squealing with delight as Marilyn pushes her up and up.

Then it's Christine's turn and I push her until she gets used to leaning back, bending her knees, stretching out her feet, powering herself higher and higher till she's able to see over the hedge, over the fields, down to the sea.

"That was brilliant!" she laughs, as the swing gradually slows to a stop and she hops off.

We spend the rest of the morning taking turns on the swing and playing hide and seek round the garden, from time to time bumping into Dad and Uncle Sandy as they wander along the paths, on a tour of inspection among the rows of vegetables and fruit. I watch Uncle Sandy puffing on his pipe and hear him say how difficult it is to grow things in his garden because of the salt spray that blows in on the wind from the sea.

Mum calls us in for dinner and we run to wash our hands and sit down at the table in the dining room. We usually eat in the kitchen but today there's too many of us. Mum has pulled out all the leaves on the big oak table, spread her best white linen tablecloth and set out twelve places with cutlery from the sideboard. Aunt Jemima helps her serve plates of stew and dumplings, with new potatoes and carrots from the garden.

# The Railway

A steam engine crossing Muchalls Viaduct

As soon as dinner is over, Eric asks,
"Can we go and see the trains?"
"Yes, please," say Joy and Christine. "Can we go now?"
So off we go, down the Manse Road, past the school, through the wooden gate and onto the platform at the station. Mr Caird, the stationmaster, smiles at us.

"The London train is due in five minutes," he says. "Remember to stand well back because it'll be going very fast."

So we sit on one of the bench seats on the platform, swinging our legs, and wait. We see the footbridge that crosses the rail tracks and the tubs of pink and red geraniums outside the waiting room. We watch the silhouette of the signalman high up in his glass box as he pulls the lever and listen to the faint clank of the signal further up the line as it falls into position, giving permission for the train to come through. We sit quietly and wait. Soon we feel the vibration along the rail track, and hear the distant rumble of the engine getting louder and louder until, with a cloud of smoke and a hiss of steam, the train bursts out of the cutting at Findon and hurtles down the track from Aberdeen, whizzing past us in a blast of air and a blur of wheels and pistons and coaches, squeezing under the road bridge below the church. We watch the red lights swaying at the back of the guards van, dancing into the distance till they fade from view.

We turn to look at the smiling, wide-eyed faces of the Shetlanders. We are used to the trains passing through Portethen but there are no trains where they live and so for them this is strange and very exciting.

"Can we watch the next train from the bridge?" asks Christine.

"Yes, of course," says Stuart, and we walk sedately along the platform and through the gate, then run as fast as we can up the cinder track, past the stationmaster's house, past the row of rail workers' cottages, past the signal box to the bridge over the track next to Mrs Thompson's shop. We lean over the parapet and listen. After a few minutes we hear the faint sound of an engine coming along the line from Stonehaven and see the train round the bend, smoke belching out of its funnel, struggling to pull a fleet of wagons behind it. We watch as the train approaches the bridge and hear a piercing whistle. The engine driver has spotted us and is leaning out of his cab giving us a wave. We wave back then run across the road, smothered in a cloud of smoke, to lean over the parapet and count the wagons, piled high with coal, as they pass underneath us.

"One, two, three," we count out loud.

"Eighteen, nineteen, twenty," we chorus and think it's no wonder the engine is going so slowly, huffing and puffing as it drags its heavy load. And still they come.

"Twenty eight, twenty nine, thirty wagons," we count, listening to the clickety clack of the wheels on the track and metallic clanking of the chains that link the wagons together. We hear the sounds grow fainter and fainter as the procession grinds its way up the slope, over the bridge near the old mill and disappears into the rock-lined cutting at Findon.

We walk home, and Eric, Joy and Christine rush to tell their Mum and Dad about all the things they've seen - the man in the signal box, the passengers in the London train whizzing past, the engine driver who blew his whistle and waved to us, the number of coal wagons being pulled by one engine.

At nighttime, we climb the stairs to bed. We need to be quiet because baby Ronald is already asleep in a cot in the front bedroom. Eric is sleeping on a camp bed in Stuart's room; Joy and Christine are sharing a bedroom with Marilyn and I. Sandra is in a little bed in Mum and Dad's room. We are all so excited that we don't feel tired.

"I'll not be able to sleep for the noise of the trains," says Joy.

We look at her in surprise. We never even notice them passing along the line at night.

"Can we see if there are any trains now?" asks Eric.

So we tiptoe to the window of Stuart's bedroom, pull aside the curtains and peer out into the darkness. We stand quietly and wait. After a few minutes we hear the distant growl of a steam engine and see a faint red glow seeping from the footplate. Suddenly there is a whoosh, and up into the night sky shoots a plume of sparks.

"What was that?" gasps Eric.

"That's what happens when the fireman opens the furnace door and throws in a shovelful of coal," explains Stuart.

We watch until the last glimmer of light disappears and the clickety-clack sound of the wheels on the line fades into silence. We go to bed and fall asleep, with the sound of the trains weaving in and out of our dreams.

# Aberdeen Beach

Marilyn, Rev Alexander Dunn, Joy Pearson, Elizabeth and Sandra
on the promenade at Aberdeen Beach

Next morning the sun is shining and we jump out of bed, get dressed, eat our breakfast and go out to play. Stuart and Eric get the bikes out of the garage and set off for a cycle run over to Findon. I show Joy and Christine the best climbing tree in the wood and tell them which branches to hold on to till they reach the top. Sandra takes them to her den among the snowberry bushes where she plays houses with her dolls. Marilyn shows them her secret hiding place in the drystane dyke where she keeps the precious things she finds - pieces of coloured glass and painted china, a shiny pebble, a special feather. She lays them on a bed of dark green moss, and then hides them behind a stone in the dyke so that no one else knows where to find them. We play around the garden and courtyard until Mum calls us in for dinner. Just as we're munching our way through the last strawberry on our plate, Dad asks.

"Who'd like to go to Aberdeen Beach?"

"Me! Me!" we chorus.

"Can we go on the dodgems?" asks Stuart.

Dad looks at Uncle Sandy with a twinkle in his eye, and they pretend that maybe not, then they're laughing and we know the answer is, "Yes". So, once everyone's finished their dinner, off we go in two cars, along the main road past Findon and the Loch of Loirston, over the River Dee, past the harbour and down to the boulevard that runs along parallel to the sea. Dad parks our car opposite the Beach Ballroom. Uncle Sandy swings in next to him and we all tumble out and skip along the promenade till we come to the Funfair.

"We'll all go on the dodgems," says Dad, "but you can each pick one other ride."

"I'm going on the Gallopers," I say.

"That's too slow," says Stuart. "I'm going on the Waltzers. Coming, Eric?"

"I'll go with Stuart and Eric," says Uncle Sandy. "Meet you at the dodgems."

Dad leads the way to the Gallopers. I love everything about this ride. I love the horses with their outstretched hooves leaping over imaginary hurdles. I love their smiley faces and pricked-up ears, the shiny gold paint on their bits and bridles, and the bright pink and blue swirling patterns round their necks and saddles. I love the way they move, lurching up and down, round and round, but not so fast that it makes you dizzy.

"Elizabeth, take Sandra with you," says Dad, and I take her hand as we climb the steps onto the platform. I lift her up onto the front saddle and tell her to hold onto the horse's neck. I sit behind holding the twisted brass pole. Marilyn climbs onto a horse next to us and Joy and Christine share one just behind. Dad pays the man in charge and off we go. The music from the fairground organ begins to play and, as we circle round, I watch the concertina of cardboard with its punched holes feeding into the machine and an invisible hand reaching out to bang the drums and clang the cymbals. I listen to the puffs of air singing from the pipe organ as we gallop forward, rising and falling, as if we were on a real horse. I see Marilyn waving to Dad each time she passes him and Joy and Christine laughing and pointing to Eric and Stuart swinging round and round on the Waltzers.

After a few minutes, I can feel our ride beginning to slow down, as if the horses were struggling to leap the hurdles. Gradually it slows to a stop and we jump down and go to join Dad.

"Did you enjoy that?" he asks.

"Yes, yes," we chorus.

We wait for the boys to join us then wend our way through the stalls to the dodgems. This is Dad and Stuart's favourite ride but I'm not so sure about it. Dad climbs into a red car with Sandra, wrapping a protective arm round her to keep her safe. Uncle Sandy has Christine with him and is letting her steer. Joy is a passenger in Eric's car. I hop into the driving seat of a blue car with Marilyn next to me. Stuart has a car all to himself. Off we go, slowly at first, with a scrape of the pole against the ceiling and a shower of sparks. I drive sedately round in a clockwise direction, doing my best to keep out of trouble. Eric has his foot flat on the floor and, suddenly, there is a bump and I'm thrown forward. I look over my shoulder and Eric is there, grinning from ear to ear. Then there is a bang and Stuart crashes into us. Eric swings his car round and sets off in pursuit and from then on it is chaos. Stuart and Eric drive against the flow of traffic, deliberately ramming anyone who comes near, crashing into the side of me and Marilyn, pushing us into a snarl of cars where we have to be rescued by a young man, leaping onto the bumper, twisting the steering wheel and sending us on our way. We're jolted and thrown around while the men folk laugh and look like they're having great fun. I breathe a sigh of relief when the ride is over and we can climb out, but don't say anything because I can see everyone one else has had a good time.

We walk slowly towards the exit, stopping to watch someone trying to knock a coconut off a shelf. Marilyn and Christine wander on ahead, then come rushing back full of excitement.

"Can we go and see the fat lady and the little lady?" asks Christine.

"What? Where?" asks Uncle Sandy.

"There's a man over there with a megaphone," says Christine, "and he's calling out,

*"Roll up, roll up to see the fat lady.*

*When she coughs she spits*

*And when she spits she wets the carpet."*

"Are you sure that's what he's saying?" asks Uncle Sandy, doubtfully.

"Yes, yes," says Christine and Marilyn nods. "Please, please can we go and see the fat lady and the little lady? It's only a penny."

The rest of us are curious and think it sounds interesting and so Uncle Sandy, very reluctantly, gives us each a penny and off we go. We pay the man at the entrance, squeeze through a velvet curtain and there, sitting in an armchair on a raised platform, in the spotlight, is the fattest lady I have ever seen. I'm too shy to stare at her face but I see a bracelet almost lost among rolls of flesh on a bare pink arm. I think to myself,

"How does anyone get to be so fat?"

We're all as skinny as rakes in our family, no matter how much we eat. I remember what Christine said the man with the megaphone called and wait, expectantly, but the lady neither coughs nor spits. She just glances at us and looks bored.

Next to her on the platform is the little lady, not even as tall as Sandra who's only four years old. The little lady has dark, wavy hair and she's dressed in a pretty floral dress and high-heeled shoes. She's sitting on a stool, playing a tune on a miniature piano. She looks up and smiles at me.

"Hello, dearie," she says.

"Hello," I reply.

I want to ask her lots of questions,

"What is the tune you're playing? Where did you learn to play the piano? Why are you so small? Are you a dwarf like in the story of Snow White and the Seven Dwarves?" but I keep quiet because I don't want to sound rude.

Silently we file past the two ladies and stumble out through the curtains, back into daylight, where Dad and Uncle Sandy are waiting.

"Well, how was it?" asks Dad.

I'm not sure what to say because it made me feel uncomfortable seeing people who looked so odd and knowing we were paying to stare at them. But Eric is telling his Dad all about what he's seen and that he's never come across anybody like that in Shetland. I'm thinking that I've never come across anybody like that in Portlethen.

We make our way out of the Funfair, stop at the edge of the pavement to watch out for traffic, then cross the road, skip down the steps and onto the beach. The tide is out leaving behind miles and miles of sand. We sit down and take off our socks and shoes, then run down to the sea, jumping over the waves, squealing as the ice cold water laps round our ankles. We find a piece of driftwood and use it to write our names in the damp sand near the tide line. We gather shells and pebbles and bring our treasures back to show

Dad and Uncle Sandy who are leaning back on their elbows on the sand beside our pile of socks and shoes, watching the ships out at sea queuing up to enter the harbour when the tide turns.

Stuart starts scooping up sand to make a sandcastle. We all join in, using our hands because we haven't brought a bucket and spade. We surround the castle with a moat and decorate the battlements with shells and seaweed.

After a while, I see Dad looking at his watch and know he is thinking that it's nearly time to go home.

"Anyone want an ice cream?" he asks. "Right, on with your socks and shoes and let's go."

We rub our feet dry, sliding our fingers between our toes to get the sand out. We put on our socks and shoes, jump to our feet and follow Dad across the road and into the Washington Café. We always buy our ice creams here when we come to the beach at Aberdeen and so the man behind the counter greets Dad like an old friend. Dad orders sliders for everyone. We watch as the man slips a crispy wafer into a silvery metal holder, places a scoop of vanilla ice cream on top, adds another wafer, then slides it on to a sheet of shiny paper on the counter. When he's made one for everyone, Dad and Uncle Sandy pay for them and carry them carefully outside. We cross the road, find a bench seat facing out to sea and wait while Dad hands out the sliders. We gently squeeze the wafers, and run our tongues round the ice cream as it oozes out, catching the creamy drops before they melt. It tastes scrumptious. We nibble a corner of the crunchy wafer, lick a mouthful of ice cream, round and round till the wafer gets soft and squelchy and the last drop of ice cream melts and disappears. We wipe our mouths with the back of our hands and think that is the very best way to end an afternoon at the seaside.

# Portlethen Church

The next day is Sunday and so we all get ready to go to church. We have to lend Joy and Christine hats to wear because it's the rule that men have to take their hats off when they go into church but women and girls have to wear a hat. We walk together down the Manse Road, round past the Post Office and the Jubilee Hall, over the railway bridge and up the steep path that leads to the church door. We go inside and squash into the Manse pew. We sit quietly and watch as Dad walks slowly in from the vestry, head bowed, and climbs the steps to the pulpit.

"Doesn't Uncle Alec look serious?" murmurs Christine. She's used to seeing him laughing and joking in his old brown tweed suit, not being solemn in his black minister's gown.

We start by singing the first hymn,

"Summer suns are glowing

Over land and sea."

"The sun always shines in Portlethen," whispers Joy.

I think to myself, "Hm. Not sure if that's true. Perhaps it's sunnier and warmer here than in Shetland, but not on the days when the haar drifts in from the North Sea and we hear the foghorn at Girdleness grumbling through the cold, damp gloom. Not much sign of a 'glowing' sun then!"

When the service is over, we go into the vestry and watch while Dad takes off his gown and his cassock and hangs them in the cupboard. Then we all go home for Sunday lunch and eat the chicken that has been slowly roasting in the oven while we've been away.

In the afternoon we play in the garden but we tell the Shetlanders that we have to play quietly on a Sunday. We can't shout and run about. We can't skip or play with a ball, and it's not just us children that have to follow the rules. Mum can't knit on a Sunday and she can't hang the washing out, even though it's a good drying day. When we ask why, Mum explains that it says in the Bible,

"Remember the Sabbath day to keep it holy."

We're the minister's family, and so we have to set a good example.

# The Double Decker Bus

The next day, we all wake up bright and early and clatter downstairs to the kitchen for breakfast.

"What are we going to do today?" asks Stuart.

"Well, I've got to go visiting at the hospital," says Dad, "So your Uncle Sandy is in charge."

Uncle Sandy sets down his cup of tea and looks round at us all.

"What would you like to do today?" he asks.

"Can we go to the swimming pool in Stonehaven?" asks Eric.

"Yes, yes," chorus Joy and Christine.

I catch Marilyn's eye and we look glumly at each other. Oh dear! I know a trip to a swimming pool is a treat for the Shetlanders because there is no swimming pool where they are, not even in Lerwick. We've heard stories about how they learned to swim with their water wings in the wild Atlantic Ocean. We learned in the beautifully warm, indoor pool at Crieff Hydro where we go on holiday every year. So a trip to the chilly, seawater pool at Stonehaven with its cold, draughty changing rooms is a bit of an ordeal. Still, the little Shetlanders are our guests and so, if they want to go, we won't complain.

"Can we go on the bus?" asks Christine.

"We'll have to," answers Uncle Sandy, "because we'll not all squeeze into my car."

So Mum and Aunt Jemima help us roll up our swimming costumes and bathing caps inside towels and make sure we have money for our bus fare. Little Ronnie is not going but he's got Magnus, our dog, to play with so he's quite happy.

We walk up the Manse Road, stand at the bus stop on the main Aberdeen road and wait. It's not long before we see a bus making its way down the slope at Hillside.

"It's a double decker," shouts Eric.

Joy and Christine jump up and down with excitement. They don't have double decker buses in Shetland.

"Can we go upstairs?" asks Joy. Uncle Sandy smiles and nods and says, Yes, but he'll probably stay downstairs.

The bus comes to a stop and we clamber up onto the platform at the rear and climb the stairs to the top deck. As the bus sets off, we wobble our way to the front and squeeze onto the bench seats where we have the best view. As the bus rounds the bend past Tawse's Smiddy, we hear footsteps clumping up the stairs and there's the bus conductress in her navy uniform and peaked hat saying,

"Fares, please."

Stuart hands her his money.

"Return to Stonehaven, please," he says.

She takes his money and drops it into her brown leather shoulder bag. She twists the dials on her ticket machine.

"One child return to Stonehaven," she says, turning the handle and, with a metallic grating sound, out pops a pink paper ticket. Stuart takes his ticket and slides it carefully into his pocket to keep it safe for the return journey. Each of us in turn does the same. I can see Christine is watching, fascinated.

"Look at the different coloured tickets," she says.

"There's different colours depending on whether you are an adult or a child, or want a single or return," I explain. "Don't you have the same system in Shetland?"

"We don't have a conductress on any of our buses. The driver takes the fare," she says.

What a surprise! I've never been in a bus that doesn't have either a conductor or conductress. How can one person take the fares at the same time as driving the bus? Does the driver have to get out of his cab at each stop and come into the bus to collect the fares? The journey must be very slow. I turn to ask Christine and Joy how it works but they are watching a train chugging across Muchalls Viaduct and I don't like to interrupt. Soon we're driving through the trees in the Den o' Logie and speeding down the hill toward Stonehaven with it's rows of red sandstone houses and hotels over-looking the harbour.

# Stonehaven Open Air Swimming Pool

SWIMMING POOL, STONEHAVEN                                    D 5477

The bus stops outside the Swimming Pool and we tumble down the stairs and out onto the pavement, clutching our rolled up towels under our arms. We skip along the path, past the children's paddling pool, and wait at the cashier's desk at the entrance for Uncle Sandy to buy the tickets. Stuart and Eric head off into the Men's Changing rooms on the left while we file through the door on the right, into the Ladies' Changing Room. Uncle Sandy goes through the door marked "Spectators" to find a seat on a bench in the sun and puff on his pipe as he watches the swimmers splashing around in the pool.

We collect a wire basket from the desk, find a cubicle, draw the plastic curtain and change into our costumes, tucking our hair up under our bathing caps. I help Sandra get changed and blow up her inflatable ring because she hasn't learned to swim yet. We hand our baskets with our clothes in at the desk, collect a token which we pin to our bathing suits and follow each other out to the poolside. We can see Stuart and Eric already in the water, swimming about, splashing each other, ducking and diving, resurfacing with a splutter and a laugh and a shake of wet hair.

I make my way to the metal ladder at the shallow end and step down until I can dabble my toes in the water. It's freezing! I hesitate until I realise it's not much warmer out of the water: the sun's shining but there's a chilly wind blowing in from the North Sea over the wall surrounding the pool. So I grit my teeth and take another step, and another, wincing as the cold water sucks the warmth out of my body. I stand waist deep, wrapping my arms round myself to try and stop my teeth chattering, and watch Marilyn climb gingerly down the ladder to join me. We both turn to help Sandra down the steps and watch as she bobs off happily in her ring. Joy and Christine are sitting on the edge of the pool, feet dangling in the water. I hear Joy say, "One, two, three, go," and see them drop down with a splash and a squeal at the shock of the sudden cold. Marilyn and I join hands and jump up and down, ducking a little lower each time until the water reaches our necks.

"Right, that's me under," I say to myself. "Now, I wonder if I can remember how to swim. It's a long time since I was last in the pool at Crieff Hydro. Let's hope it's like riding a bike and you never forget."

I stretch out along the water and launch into my best breaststroke. I'd forgotten that the water in Stonehaven Swimming Pool is seawater, so salty that it makes you much more buoyant than the freshwater pool at Crieff. I swim till I reach the far side then turn on my back. I float effortlessly, watching the clouds drifting overhead, listening to the quiet gurgle of the water round my ears. This is wonderful. I am starting to enjoy myself. I turn over and swim back to join the others. Marilyn is kicking her legs like a frog, pushing Sandra in the ring in front of her. Joy and Christine are racing each

# STONEHAVEN SWIMMING POOL and PADDLING POOL

Heated, Open-Air, Sea Water Swimming Pool filtered and sterilised by the most up-to-date process in the world.

other from one side of the pool to the other. I expect they are thinking that this is a lot safer place to go bathing than among the waves and currents and sharp rocks in the sea off Shetland.

"We're going to go down the slide," shouts Stuart. "Want to come?"

We shake our heads. The slide is at the deep end, next to the diving board. None of us girls are confident enough to go out of our depths, to somewhere where you can't reach the bottom and stand up if you want to. We stay at the shallow end, swimming round in circles, racing from side to side, holding onto the edge and splashing our feet, and watching from a distance as Stuart and Eric hurtle down the slide. Uncle Sandy waits patiently, smiling and waving to us every now and again, until at last he points at his watch to let us know its time to get out because we need to get the bus home.

We make our way back into the changing room and stand shivering while we hand over our tokens and wait to collect our baskets of clothes. I take Sandra into the changing cubicle with me, wrap her in a towel and tell her to dry herself. I struggle to dress myself with fingers turning white and numb with cold and remember why I always have mixed feelings about going swimming. I hate the shock of going into cold water at the beginning. I enjoy the swimming in the middle, but then I hate the bit at the end, trying to get dry, struggling to slide socks back onto feet that are still damp, and button up cardigans and tie shoelaces with fingers that are numb with cold.

Eventually, we all get dressed again, wring out our bathing costumes, roll them in damp towels, and go to join Uncle Sandy.

"Well, did you enjoy that?" he asks.

"Yes, yes," we answer. "That was great fun."

He buys us all an ice cream and we sit in the sun and laugh as we lick all round the cone and catch the drops on our tongues before they melt. When we have popped the last morsel into our mouths and wiped our sticky hands on our damp towels, we leave the Swimming Pool and catch the bus back to Portlethen.

So the days go by in a flurry of activity: there are walks across Portlethen Moss to inspect the peat bank, visits to the castles along Deeside, picnics at the beach, singing and play-acting concerts in the evening. I lie in bed at night and listen to the sound of laughter dancing up the stairs from the drawing room below, and feel happy that our serious, hard-working Mum and Dad are having fun and enjoying the company of their friends from Shetland.

# Departure

T hen the day comes when the holiday is over and it's time for the Shetlanders to go home. There's an afternoon spent packing suitcases, loading the luggage into the boot of the Pearsons' car, saying cheerio to the cats, the hens, the rabbits, the dog, before we all drive to Aberdeen harbour to see our visitors off on the overnight sailing to Lerwick. Uncle Sandy drives their car onto the quayside where it waits to be hoisted on board. We park in the street nearby and go to join them. We all make our way gingerly up the sloping gangway, holding on to the sides, trying not to look over the handrail at the dark water below us. We follow Uncle Sandy down the steep wooden stairway to their cabin, listening to the thrum of the engines as the ship gets ready to sail.

"Come and we'll show you around," says Eric, and we leave the grown-ups stowing the overnight bags under the bunk beds and follow him along the corridors. We peer into the dining room and the lounges, and climb the stairs and out on to the bow, tripping over ropes and anchor chains, leaning over the railings to watch the hustle and bustle on the quayside, listening to the creak of the hawsers as they tug impatiently on the capstans.

Marilyn pulls my sleeve and whispers anxiously,

"When is it time to get off? What if they take away the gangway and we get stuck on board and have to go to Shetland?"

Just then, there's a loud blast from the ship's siren and we hear a sailor shouting for everyone who isn't sailing tonight to leave the ship. We hurry to the top of the gangway and there's Mum tearfully hugging Aunt Jemima and little Ronnie, and Dad shaking hands with Uncle Sandy amid cries of "Thank you for a wonderful holiday," and "Safe journey home," and "Come again soon."

I can feel Marilyn fidgeting beside me and know she's watching the procession of visitors leaving the ship and wishing Mum and Dad would hurry up. Finally, the farewells are over and we walk carefully back down the gangway and stand on the quayside watching as the last car is hoisted on board and the hold battened down to make it watertight. Smoke is belching out of the funnel as the engines start to drive the propellers, churning up the water at the stern of the ship. Dockers untie the hawsers, dropping them with a splash into the sea, and the ship pushes back from the quay and starts to turn towards the harbour entrance.

"Quick," says Dad, "Back to the car," and we turn and run over the rough, granite setts, climb in and slam the doors. Dad drives as fast as he can round the edge of the harbour, along the road towards the breakwater that stretches its long finger out into the sea. We clamber out and follow Dad past the Customs House, past the Pilots' station, out towards the lighthouse at the far end. We watch as the St Clair glides by, scanning the row of passengers leaning over the rail, waving frantically, hoping our little family of visitors can see us. We stand together, quietly, long after the ship has left the harbour, watching as it reaches the open ocean and starts to dip up and down in the swell and, as the evening sun sets, we see it grow smaller and smaller, heading north until it disappears below the horizon.

We go home to a house that is oddly quiet and subdued. We miss the sound of lilting voices, and the chatter and laughter. We miss sharing our world with other people. We miss the Shetlanders.

# August

Beith Boys Brigade marching past Mrs Thompson's Shop and over the railway bridge on their way to a service at Portlethen Church

# Shopping

It's Saturday morning and Marilyn and I are going shopping for Mum. I'm carrying the purse with the money and the list of messages. Marilyn is carrying the Ration Book and the wicker basket. We walk along the road past the Jubilee Hall, past the schoolhouse, past the Crichton's bungalow, round the corner near the railway bridge, through the granite gateposts and into the gravel courtyard in front of Mrs Thompson's shop.

We pause to peer in through the shop window. Along the sides are boxes of biscuits, cans of fruit and packets of soap flakes, but in the centre is an enticing display of sweets. There are jars of black liquorice comfits, red and white striped Berwick Cockles and rainbow-coloured gobstoppers that turn your tongue red and yellow and blue. There are tubes of sherbet dab that you suck up through a liquorice straw until it makes you sneeze or gives you a coughing fit. There are Parma Violets wrapped in shiny cellophane paper, bars of Cow Candy, and boxes of Rowntrees Fruit Gums. We get threepence a week pocket money and need to buy something which will last as long as possible, and so I usually get four sticks of liquorice, which cost a penny, and tuppence worth of yellow fizzy sherbet. If you suck the liquorice stick then dip it into the sherbet, you can taste the lemon and the liquorice at the same time when you pop it in your mouth. It is delicious!

Today, however, we're not here to buy sweets. We're here to shop for Mum because Mum bakes on a Saturday morning and she needs some ingredients for her recipes. So, reluctantly, we turn away from the window and push open the heavy, wooden shop door. Above our heads, we hear a bell clanging loudly, ding-a-ling, as we step up over the granite threshold and onto the creaky, wooden floorboards of a dark, gloomy room, with daylight filtering in through the net curtains at the window. The door slams shut behind us. In front of us is a high, mahogany counter and shelves stacked to the ceiling with tins and jars and boxes. The shop is full of the smells of dried tealeaves and soap and tobacco. We huddle together, whispering to each other as we open the purse and bring out the shopping list. We stand and wait, listening to the slow tick tock of a clock on the wall behind us.

After a minute or two, we hear footsteps echoing along a corridor and then, with a swish of brass rings, the green velvet curtain is swept aside and, through the doorway and into the shop, comes Mrs Thompson, grey hair tied up in a bun, floral apron crossed over her chest and tied around her waist. She peers over the counter at us with only the hint of a smile. Somehow, I always feel she regards customers coming to her shop as a bit of a nuisance, interrupting her when she's in the middle of cooking her dinner, or reading the newspaper, nicely settled in the comfortable armchair in front of her fire. Perhaps she is particularly irritated by children, clutching their pennies, taking ages deciding what to buy. Marilyn's friend, Jacqui Wright told us that she once found a farthing lying on the road and went into Mrs Thompson's shop and asked for one chew, the kind that cost four for a penny, and Mrs Thompson spoke to her very crossly, saying what a nuisance she was expecting to be served when she was spending only a farthing. And I've never forgotten the time I was bullied by some big lads into going to buy sweets for them when they'd used up their ration and couldn't buy any more sweets themselves. I remember Mrs Thompson looking sternly at me and asking,

"Are these for yourself?" I nodded my head.

"You're not buying sweets for someone else, are you?"

"No," I lied even though Mum and Dad have taught us always to tell the truth. Ever since that day, I've felt guilty whenever Mrs Thompson looks at me, thinking she's remembering and she's going to accuse me of something dreadful.

She looks at me now and holds out her hand. Nervously, I pass her Mum's list of messages. She peers at it through her round, horn-rimmed spectacles.

"Three pounds of plain flour," she reads, and turns to plunge a scoop into a sack behind the counter, tipping the flour into a brown paper bag. We watch the dust particles dancing in the beam of light from the window as she carries the bag to the counter, sets it onto one side of the scales, places a brass weight on the other side and adds flour to the bag till it slowly sinks down and the scales balance. She lifts the bag off the scales, dunts it on the counter to settle the flour and we watch her carefully fold the brown paper over and over again, then tie it with string to seal it. She takes a pencil from a drawer and writes the price of the flour on Mum's shopping list.

"Two pounds of sugar," she reads next and we watch her weighing out the sugar into another brown paper bag and noting down the price.

"A pound of raisins. Is your mother baking fruit scones this morning?" asks Mrs Thompson, looking at Marilyn. She knows that

Mum bakes every Saturday morning and that it's Marilyn who helps her.

"She's making rock buns," answers Marilyn.

Mrs Thompson purses her lips. I imagine she's thinking,

"Hmm, not a good idea. Mrs Dunn would be much better baking fruit scones."

She carries on weighing and measuring, noting down the prices until she's reached the bottom of the list. We watch her lips moving silently as she adds up the columns of pounds, shillings and pence, starting at the top, moving down the list, then counting it again from the bottom upwards to check it's correct. She tells me how much it comes to and I give her the Ration Book and money from Mum's purse. She takes the notes and coins and rattles them into the drawer under the counter, hands me some change, tears some coupons out of the Ration Book, packs the bags into our basket and stands watching, hands on her hips, as we turn to leave.

"Thank you," we say, politely. Mrs Thompson nods in reply.

"Mind the step," she says.

We hear the bell clanging above our heads as we pull the door open and let it bang shut behind us, stepping out of the gloom into the bright sunlight. We both take hold of the handle of the basket, sharing its weight, swinging it between us as we walk along the road, feeling much happier now that we've done the shopping and are on the way home.

"Thank goodness we don't have to go there every day," I say and Marilyn nods, though I know that Mrs Thompson likes Marilyn more than most children. I'm just pleased that there are lots of things we don't have to buy in Mrs Thompson's shop and think about them as I walk along.

We don't have to buy our milk from the shop because we fetch it every day in a pail from Balquharn Farm. We keep hens and so we don't have to buy eggs or a chicken for roasting on Sunday. We don't have to buy our bread from Mrs Thompson because Mitchell and Muil's van calls at the Manse twice a week. We buy mince and steak and sausages from the Butcher's van on Tuesday and fish from Mr Duncan's van on Friday.

We don't have to buy vegetables because we grow all our own in the garden. During the summer, there are always new potatoes and peas-in-the- pod and lettuce for salads, and, when the autumn comes, Dad buries the potatoes and the carrots in a clamp, lined with straw, so that they keep over the winter. Mum occasionally buys apples and oranges from one of the vans, but during the summer there's all kinds of fruit growing in the garden and Mum makes lots of jam to eat over the winter. We go bramble picking along the roadside in autumn and Mum boils the fruit and fills lots of jars with bramble jelly. One year the WRI, that's the Women's Rural Institute, hired a canning machine and Mum spent a whole day boiling pears and then using the machine to seal them into tin cans. I'm not sure it was a great success or worth the effort because the canning machine never reappeared.

We certainly never buy flowers because there's always something growing in the garden. There are roses and lupins and marigolds in summer, gladioli and dahlias in autumn, daffodils and lilies in spring. It's one of my jobs on a Saturday morning to bring in bunches of flowers and arrange them in vases in the drawing room, in case we have visitors, and when Mum is invited to a wedding with Dad, she doesn't have to buy flowers for her buttonhole because we make her a spray of roses or sweet peas or lily-of-the-valley, wrapping their stems in silver paper. I remember there was one year, just after the War, when we even sold some of the flowers from the garden. We helped Mum to pick bunches of the daffodils that grow along the edge of the garden paths, and tie them in bundles so that she could sell them to a flower shop in Aberdeen.

Every year, at the start of the season, the local salmon fishermen give the minister one of the first fish caught in their nets. Two of Dad's elders are salmon fishermen: Mr Main is skipper of the Portlethen cobble, and Mr Wood is the skipper of the cobble that goes out from the harbour at the Downies. So, once a year, they come to the door with a freshly caught salmon, trussed up in green rushes, tied with string. There's great excitement as Mum gets the tin salmon kettle out from the bottom shelf in the scullery, fills it with water and cooks the salmon on the stove. The whole house fills with the smell of fish as it's lifted out and laid on the blue and white china ashet on the kitchen table. That night there's fresh salmon salad for tea, with new potatoes and lettuce and parsley and chives from the garden. The next day, Mum uses the leftovers to bake a "Salmon Fondue" which she only makes on special occasions. She mixes butter, flour, egg yolks and flakes of salmon and then beats egg whites till they're stiff, folds them into the mixture and bakes it in a Pyrex dish in the oven till it's golden brown on top. When it's ready, Mum lifts it out of the oven and sets it in the middle of the table with great ceremony. As usual, Dad says the grace,

"For what we are about to receive, may the Lord make us truly thankful. Amen."

Then Mum, slowly and carefully, dishes out a spoonful on to each of our plates. We taste it and we tell her it's delicious and what a good cook she is. Mum looks very pleased.

Mrs Thompson's shop doesn't sell clothes or shoes and so we have to buy them in Aberdeen. When Mum decides we girls need a new summer dress or Stuart needs new trousers, she sends Dad into Isaac Benzies in Aberdeen. The shop assistants help him pick out a selection of suitable clothes and he brings them home in the car. We try them on, one after the other, strutting about the bedroom like models on a catwalk, posing in front of the mirror until we decide which we like best. Usually Marilyn, Sandra and I get to choose a different dress but, one year, Mum decided it would be a good idea if we all dressed the same. So she bought a blue dress with white spots for each of us. The problem was that when I grew out of mine, it was handed down to Marilyn and then to Sandra who complained bitterly of spending years wearing blue, spotty dresses.

Marilyn and Sandra often have to wear hand-me-down clothes but Mum is very fussy about us always having good, well-fitting shoes. She tells us that, when she was a girl growing up in Orkney, she was the tenth child out of fourteen in her family and never had a pair of new shoes bought specially for her. She always wore hand-me-downs that often didn't fit properly and so the bones in her feet didn't get a chance to grow straight and true and have been painful all her life. She is determined that this won't happen to us, and so every once in a while, she sends us into Aberdeen with Dad to go to Clark's Shoe Shop in George Street where we get our feet measured, and sometimes X-rayed, to make sure our shoes are the correct size.

We don't often buy new books, only at birthdays and Christmas. There are lots of books in the house that belong to Dad and so we can go to a bookcase anytime and find well known stories like "Black Beauty," "Alice in Wonderland" or "Grimm's Fairy Tales." We're given books as Sunday School prizes but they're usually stories about missionaries doing good works in Africa, not always great fun to read. However, one of the highlights of our week is a visit to the lending library in John Menzies shop in Union Street in Aberdeen. Downstairs, below the main shop, is an Aladdin's cave of treasures, shelves and shelves of books with their glossy, brightly coloured covers and their wonderful new-book smell. I make straight for the Enid Blyton section. Is there a new volume in the Adventure series? I have read, "The Island of Adventure", "The Castle of Adventure," "The Valley of Adventure," all wonderful stories, so exciting. Is there a new Famous Five book? What are Julian, Dick, Anne, George and the dog, Timmy, up to this time? If I find one I haven't read, I pounce on it and take it to Dad. He waits till we've chosen our favourite books, and then arranges for us to borrow them for a week. I can hardly wait till I get home to start reading, though Mum complains that I've got my nose stuck in a book when she needs me to help her.

While I've been thinking about fresh salmon and new dresses and adventure stories, Marilyn and I have been walking home from Mrs Thompson's shop. We open the back door, set the shopping basket on the kitchen table and hand over the purse and the Ration Book. Mum checks the shopping list to make sure we've got everything, checks that Mrs Thompson has added up the cost correctly, checks that we've been given the right change, then smiles and says,

"Well done, girls. Right, we've got the flour, the sugar, the raisins. Let's get started on the baking."

I can hear the peat fire roaring in the range, heating the oven, and see the baking tins lined up, greased and waiting, the recipe book open and little sister, Sandra, standing on a chair, brandishing a wooden spoon, ready to help. Marilyn ties her apron round her waist, and Mum hands her a bowl of eggs and a whisk. I leave the bakers, dash upstairs, change into my dungarees and old jumper, run downstairs, push my feet into my wellies and go outside to join Dad in the garden.

Stuart is mowing the front lawn as I help Dad dig and wheel-barrow, hoe and rake. After a while, we hear knocking and there's Mum, sliding the sash window open, holding out a plate of newly-baked scones, dripping with melted butter and strawberry jam. Dad pulls up a battered old wooded chair, Stuart sits down on the upturned wheelbarrow and I perch on the window ledge, balancing the plate on my lap. We drink a mug of tea and munch into our scones. This is the reward for braving Mrs Thompson's shop on a Saturday morning.

# September

Rev Alexander Dunn and Mrs Florence Dunn

# Bramble Picking

It's a sunny Saturday afternoon in September and we're cycling along the Aberdeen Road, Dad at the front on his big bike with the enormous wheels, Stuart at the back on his new silver Raleigh bike with the crossbar and me in the middle on my very small, very old bike. It's the first time I've ever ridden my bike on the Main Road and I'm concentrating hard on not wobbling and hitting the kerb, particularly when a bus or a lorry whizzes past.

Dangling from the handlebars of Dad's bike are two shiny metal milk pails because we're off to pick brambles at Cairnwell. Dad loves bramble picking. All week, while we've been at school, he's been out on his bike, coming home, pleased as punch, with his pail full of brambles. At first Mum was very encouraging but, this morning, I heard her complaining that she was fed up boiling the berries, squeezing them through a muslin bag, filling up jam jars. She showed Dad her hands stained purple with the juice, and the larder shelves full to overflowing.

"Alec, we don't need any more bramble jelly. We've more than enough to last the winter," she protested, but Dad just smiled, turned to us children and asked,

"Who wants to go bramble picking?"

"Me," I shouted. Ever since I was a toddler, I have followed Dad around like a shadow, always wanting to be with him, trotting after him in the garden, standing watching him sawing and hammering at his workbench in the garage, asking to go with him wherever he went, running after his car crying, "Me too. Me too."

"Elizabeth, you're too young to cycle on the main road," said Mum. "Why don't you stay here with your sisters? We're going to do some baking."

"I want to go with Dad and Stuart," I said stubbornly.

So here I am, off on an expedition to Cairnwell, feeling happy and excited, pedalling hard to keep up with Dad.

"Stuart, Elizabeth, follow me. We're going to turn right," says Dad, sticking out his right arm, looking over his shoulder to make sure there are no cars coming. I turn my handlebars and wobble after him, swinging right onto the narrow farm track that slopes steeply between drystane dykes up to the farm of Cairnwell at the top of the hill. Dad pedals strongly and quickly pulls ahead. Stuart whizzes past me, keen to show how fast he can go on his new bike, and sets off after Dad. I'm pedalling as fast as my legs will go but am soon left far behind.

"Wait for me," I cry, but the wind carries my voice away over the fields and no one hears. I watch, panic-stricken, as Dad and Stuart get farther and farther away till they disappear round a bend behind the farm buildings, leaving me on my own. I start crying and can't see where I'm going for the tears in my eyes. Suddenly I'm in the long grass at the side of the road, the wheels of my bike tangled up in thistles and dock, and I'm tumbling, falling, crashing down with my bike on top of me, banging my elbow, scraping my knee. I scramble up, wipe the tears from my eyes with my coat sleeve, get back on my bike and set off again up the hill, desperately pedalling as fast as my legs will go.

I reach the farm, cycle round the corner and there is Dad, bike propped up against a telegraph pole, leaning on a farm gate, chatting to the farmer's wife. Stuart is sitting astride his bike, scuffing his feet on the gravel. I brake to a stop beside him. Dad looks at me and smiles, then raises his eyebrows in surprise.

"Elizabeth, are you crying? What's wrong?"

"I thought you'd gone and left me," I sniffle, not looking at him.

"Of course I wouldn't go and leave you," says Dad in amazement.

"Silly idiot," says Stuart, unsympathetically, as I wipe my eyes on my sleeve, feeling stupid and embarrassed. The farmer's wife smiles kindly at me.

"Right, off we go again," says Dad, "Stuart, you go first this time. I'll stay behind Elizabeth."

Good! Dad is at the back and so this time I won't be left behind. I feel happy again. Along the single-track road we go, past fields of black and white cows, past grass verges bright with yellow buttercups and blue speedwell, through avenues of rowan trees laden with red berries, past birch trees with golden leaves dancing in the autumn sunshine, skirting the heather-covered lower slopes of the hill that leads up to Boswell's Monument.

"Stop!" shouts Dad. "I can see some good brambles."

I brake and skid to a halt on the gravel. We lay our bikes on the grass verge and squeeze through the wire fence and into the middle of a patch of brambles, laden with purple berries. Dad hands Stuart a milk pail.

"You two pick into this pail. Elizabeth, you pick the low branches on the outside. I'll get the ones in the middle."

So we start picking. This is good fun, much better than baking

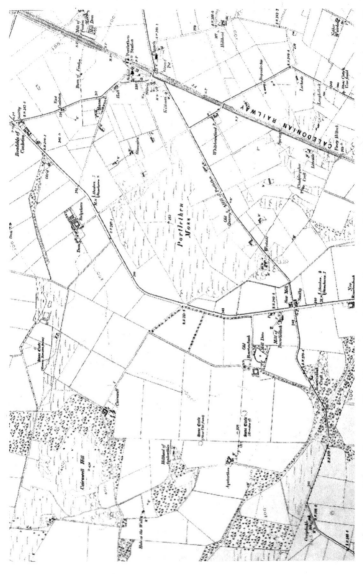

Portlethen in 1904, showing The Manse, Portlethen Moss, and the farms of Balquharn and Cairnwell.

with Mum at home. I find a really juicy bramble and pop it into my mouth instead of the pail.

"You'll never fill your pail if you keep eating them," Dad laughs.

We pick steadily, working side by side, the three of us, gathering the berries, dropping them into the milk pails.

Out of the corner of my eye, I watch Dad. I can see he is really happy. I wonder why he loves bramble picking so much. Does he like being away along some lonely road, in beautiful countryside? Does he like the idea of foraging for food for his family like men did in the olden days? Why does he always take his bike when he goes bramble picking, never his car? It's a mystery and, somehow, I can't ask him. After a while Dad says,

"I think I'm nearly done here. I'm going along the road a bit and see if I can find some more. You two finish picking here. I'll be back in a little while."

Off he goes, squeezing through the wire fence, disappearing behind the bushes. I watch anxiously but Stuart is still with me and I mustn't be a cry-baby. I go back to looking for brambles but somehow all the easy-to-find ones have disappeared. I take a step forward to reach a berry and into the path of a very prickly branch that clasps and clings round my legs, scratching them through my woollen stockings. I bend down to try to disentangle myself.

"Ouch," I cry, "I think I've got a thorn in my finger."

"Let me see," says Stuart. "Now hold still. I'll pull it out."

My finger is sore. I suck it to stop it hurting and try to be brave. I can feel my lip wobble but this time I don't cry. Minutes later I hear an "Ouch" from Stuart and see him examining a long scratch on the back of his hand. We don't have any plasters so it keeps on bleeding. We go back to picking but, without Dad's cheerful enthusiasm, it all feels difficult and uncomfortable.

The sun is dipping behind the hill and it's starting to grow dark.

"Stuart, I'm cold and I'm all scratched," I say. "I want to go home. Where's Dad gone? Can we go and look for him?"

"He'll be back soon," says Stuart, hopefully. "He said to wait here so we'd better not leave."

He pauses and I can tell he's as fed up with bramble picking as I am.

"We could go out onto the road and call him," he suggests.

We crawl through the fence and shout, "Dad, Dad," then stand quietly, listening. We hear the distant mooing of cows as they make their way into the byre for milking and the wind rustling the leaves in the trees above our heads, but no sound of Dad. We sit down on the grass beside our bikes and wait. We examine our fingers, stained purple with bramble juice, and count how many scratches we've got on our hands and arms. We wait. I huddle close to Stuart, shivering and hugging my knees, trying to keep warm. We wait. At last we hear footsteps and, along the road, strides Dad, swinging his milk pail, smiling cheerfully.

"How did you get on? Pail full?" he asks. "I found such a good patch. Do you want to see?"

He lifts the lid of his pail to show us his berries and seems so pleased that we don't have the heart to tell him we've been cold and miserable and missing him.

"Right, we'd better go home. It's getting late. Your Mum will be wondering where we are. I'll go first. Stuart, stay behind your sister and make sure she's alright."

Off he goes, a milk pail dangling from each handlebar, pedalling strongly along the road, disappearing round the bend. Stuart waits for me to clamber onto my bike, find the pedals and wobble after Dad. We turn the corner and skid to a halt. There, in the middle of the road, is Dad's bike, lying on its side, wheels spinning and, next to it, two milk pails, sitting firmly upright. There is no sign of Dad, but we spot a hole in the hawthorn hedge that runs along the side of the road. We drop our bikes and run to peer through the prickly branches. There's Dad, lying on his back in the ditch, looking very surprised.

"Goodness me! I didn't see that pothole. Went straight over the handlebars. But what about my brambles? Are they safe?"

We help pull him up onto his feet and back through the hedge.

"Well, well, isn't that lucky. Not a single bramble spilt. Right, off we go again, but let's go carefully this time and watch out for potholes."

We cycle slowly back along the track past Cairnwell, down the slope to the Main Road, hugging the kerb until we turn right onto the Manse Road. It is almost dark by the time we reach home. We leave our bikes in the garage and make our way across the courtyard, through the back door and into the warm kitchen. Marilyn and Sandra, fresh and clean and rosy cheeked, jump up and run to meet us. I can smell newly-baked scones and see plates of rock buns, and iced fairy cakes and shortbread on the table. Mum looks at us as we come in and frowns.

"Dad fell off his bike," blurts out Stuart, "and Elizabeth got a thorn in her finger and my hand's bleeding."

"But look," says Dad proudly, plonking his two pails onto the table among the baking, "we've brought you lots of beautiful brambles."

Mum barely glances at the brambles. She takes hold of my hands, examines them, and then turns towards Dad and scolds,

"This child's hands are frozen and covered in scratches. Look at Stuart, his clothes are filthy and there's blood on his shirtsleeve. Did I hear Stuart say you fell off your bike? You could have broken your neck and then what would become of us? Alec Dunn, do you hear me? BRING ME NO MORE BRAMBLES!"

# October

Elizabeth, Stuart and Marilyn Dunn with Kathleen and Sandy Milne

# Fetching Milk from the Farm

We're walking up the Manse Road, me and my friend, Kathleen Milne, on our way to fetch the milk from Balquharn Farm. Kathleen's been my friend ever since we were little. She has light brown curly hair and lots of freckles all over her face, and a twin brother called Sandy. They were born up the road in Gushetneuk just two weeks before me. We've played together ever since we were little, made dens in the Manse Wood, paddled in the burn, run around the peat banks in the Moss. We've sat next to each other in school, and now we're fetching the milk together, just as we do most days.

It's a bright, sunny autumn day with the leaves turning orange and brown on the sycamore trees in the Manse Wood and the berries hanging in scarlet bunches from the rowans along the roadside. We march along, skipping over the puddles on the road, jumping on and off the grass verge, peering over the drystane dyke into the field that runs alongside the road. This field is called the "Glebe" because it belongs to the Church, though they don't farm it themselves: they rent it out to Mr Hall, the farmer at Balquharn. This year he grew a crop of oats in it and now it's full of stubble left over from the harvest. I remember watching the binder cutting the stalks of corn, tying them into bundles, and the fun we had playing hide and seek among the stooks, burrowing under the sheaves till no one could see us. Some years, the farmer lets the grass grow and keeps cattle in the Glebe and I can stand in the drying green at The Manse and look over the fence at the cows grazing among the daisies and the buttercups, and wading through the mud to drink from the burn. I keep an eye out for the bull because everyone knows bulls can be dangerous and you must never wear anything red near a bull or it will charge. One day I was crossing the field, taking a short cut home from Cookston Cottages, and realised there was a bull amongst the cows and I was wearing a red scarf. I ran for my life and scrambled up the wall through the hedge before the bull could see me and come after me. Today there are no animals in the field, just stubble and weeds.

At the top of the Manse Road, we turn left onto the main Aberdeen road and follow the pavement till we reach the Balquharn road end. We stop at the kerb and wait till there's a gap in the traffic before crossing. We make our way up the bumpy, stony farm track, past the bothies where the young farm workers live, past the stable where they used to keep the big cart horses, past the very smelly dung heap, past the corner of the field where the brown water running off the midden feeds the hog-weed and dock and wild rhubarb till they grow as tall as plants in a jungle. We stop when we reach the bull pen. Sometimes the metal-barred gate is standing open and we know that the bull is out in the field. Today it is shut and we pause to look in, nervously keeping our distance. There's the stocky, black Aberdeen Angus bull, standing on his short, hairy legs, his big, dark eyes staring back at us through the bars. He doesn't look so scary now. In fact, I feel quite sorry for him. It must have hurt having his nose pierced by that metal ring, and how embarrassing being dragged around by your nose, particularly in front of the cows.

We say goodbye to the bull and walk on round the corner of the farm buildings, past the garden gate that leads up to the farmhouse where I can picture Mrs Hall, busy in her kitchen, baking scones and oatcakes, making butter and cheese in a churn, packing eggs into cartons for the Egg Marketing Board to collect, or doing all the other things that farmers' wives do. I've gone with Mum lots of times to visit her sisters, Aunt Mary, Aunt Annie, Aunt Nettie, Aunt Lily and Aunt Ivy, who are all farmers' wives, and that's the kind of things they've been doing. A visit to Aunt Nettie in Echt is particularly interesting because we can watch her milking the cows by hand, sitting on a stool, leaning her head against their soft bodies, squeezing the milk out of the teats into a bucket. Then, when her work outside is done and she needs a rest, she sits down at her kitchen table, lights a cigarette and does the Press and Journal crossword.

We leave the farmhouse gate behind, cross the yard and make our way to the dairy. We can see rows of shiny milk churns lined up against the wall and the machine that's used to cool the milk, but no sign of Mrs Wattie. We go to look for her. We follow the sound of pumps and motors, mingling with the gentle mooing of cows, and go through the arched doorway into the byre. There's the row of black and white Friesian cows, quietly chewing the hay in their stalls. We can smell the straw and the manure and the warm milk and hear the rhythmic thrum of the milking machines. We watch Mr Wattie, the dairyman, attach wires and tubes to the overhead rail. We hear the sucking noise as he fits the milking claws onto the cows' udders and watch the white liquid fill the glass window in the steel churn as the milk starts to flow.

We hear the sound of footsteps, and look up to see Mrs Wattie, in

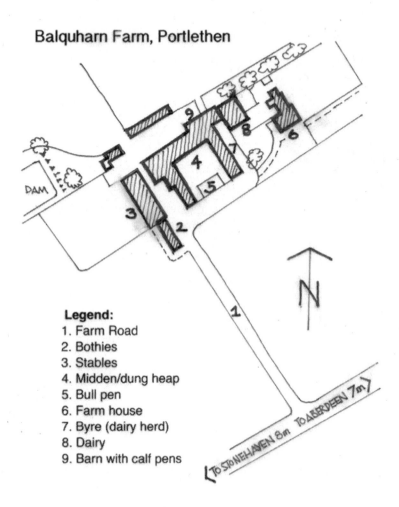

# Balquharn Farm, Portlethen

DAM

**Legend:**
1. Farm Road
2. Bothies
3. Stables
4. Midden/dung heap
5. Bull pen
6. Farm house
7. Byre (dairy herd)
8. Dairy
9. Barn with calf pens

N

To STONEHAVEN 8m    To ABERDEEN 7m

her white apron and black wellington boots, walking towards us, a steel milk bucket in each hand. She smiles and greets us,

"Hello, girls. Come for your milk?"

We follow her out of the byre, across the yard and into the dairy. We watch as she tips a bucket of warm milk into the top of the cooling machine and hear the trickle of the milk as it slowly flows down over the cold pipes and into the churn below. Mrs Wattie takes a copper ladle with a long handle and dips it into the churn. We pass her our pails and watch as she fills them up with milk. She hangs her ladle over a pipe, replaces the lids on our milk pails and hands them back to us. We're about to turn and leave when she says,

"I'm just away to feed the calves. Do you want to help me?"

"Yes, please," we answer enthusiastically. What a treat!

"Right, set your pails down there in the corner," says Mrs Wattie, pouring warm milk, straight from the cows in the byre, into some small buckets. She gives each of us one to carry and we follow her across the yard and through the doorway into a barn that's been divided up into lots of straw-filled stock pens. The nearest one is a tumbling mass of beautiful, dark-eyed, black and white calves, some frolicking among the straw bales, others mooing and calling for their mothers. When they see us, they rush to poke their heads through the wooden bars.

"Hold onto your bucket with one hand," says Mrs Wattie. "Now, stretch out your other hand and let the calf suck your fingers, then gradually lower your hand into the bucket of milk."

We do as Mrs Wattie tells us and laugh with delight when we feel a soft, pink tongue licking our fingers. We lower our hands into the buckets and listen to the squelching noise as the calves start sucking up the milk, butting their little heads against the sides, draining the last drop. I gently stroke a soft, silky ear and run my hand along a warm furry neck.

Mrs Wattie is watching us as she feeds her calf, smiling when she sees how much we are enjoying ourselves.

"Thank you, girls. You've been a great help," she says when all the buckets are empty. "You'd better get off home now or your mothers will be wondering where you are."

We say goodbye to the calves, patting their little heads for the last time. We collect our milk pails from the dairy and set off for home, chatting about how much we enjoyed feeding the calves and hoping Mrs Wattie will ask us to help her another time. We skip along the farm track, follow the pavement back along the main Aberdeen road and turn down into the Manse Road. I'm swinging my milk pail from hand to hand, then, in a fit of exuberance, put both hands together on the handle and do a little twirl, watching the pail swing out like the seats on the chair-o-planes at the fair. Kathleen laughs and copies me, whirling round and round, faster and faster, leaning back, hands outstretched, swinging her milk pail higher and higher. Disaster! The lid flies off, spinning through the air, clattering and clanging along the stony track till it comes to rest on the grass verge. Out spills a flood of milk in a circle of white, splashing over the road, over Kathleen's shoes, her skirt, her coat. The colour drains from her face behind the freckles as she slows to a stop, staring in dismay at her dripping wet clothes and the empty milk pail. Her lip wobbles and she looks like she's going to cry. I stand beside her, my milk pail hanging heavy in my hand, shocked, knowing my friend is in trouble. I walk along the road, pick up the lid, walk back and hand it to her. She fits it back onto the pail and we turn and trudge silently down the road till we reach the Milne's gate.

"I'll come in with you," I say and we walk along the garden path, push open the back door and go into the kitchen.

Mrs Milne listens as Kathleen stutters and stumbles through her story about what happened to the milk and then scolds us for being irresponsible. We hang our heads and say nothing. I'm not surprised that Mrs Milne is very cross. Milk is food for the family and costs money. Money is precious and can't be wasted. She tells Kathleen that she has to go back up to Balquharn and get some more milk.

Without a word we turn and leave. I hide my milk pail among the grass at the roadside, and then Kathleen and I set off up the road, back to Balquharn. We run part of the way because the sun is going down and it's getting dark. We have to explain to Mrs Wattie what happened and ask her to refill the Milne's pail. She tuts a bit but she can see we're miserable and so doesn't scold us. We walk carefully home, no skipping and dancing this time and definitely no twirling round. I leave Kathleen at her gate, pick up my milk pail and walk on down the Manse Road. Into my mind comes something that Dad read from the Bible in church last Sunday,

"To everything there is a season, and a time to every purpose under the heaven:

A time to weep, and a time to laugh; a time to mourn, and a time to dance;

A time to get, and a time to lose; a time to keep, and a time to cast away."

Perhaps I need to remember that when I'm carrying the family's milk supply home it is more a time of "getting" and "keeping" and not a time for "losing" and "casting away," and certainly not a time for "laughing" and "dancing."

I open the back door and go into the warm kitchen. Everyone is sitting round the table ready for tea. Mum smiles and reaches out a hand to take the milk pail from me.

"There you are, Elizabeth. You've been a long time. We were beginning to think you were lost."

"We stayed to feed the calves," I answer, hanging up my coat behind the door, sitting down on my chair at the table.

I'm remembering another bit that Dad read from the Bible,

"There is a time to keep silent, and a time to speak."

This was definitely a time to keep silent.

# November

Rev Alexander Dunn leading a Remembrance Day Service at
the War Memorial outside Portlethen Church

# Remembrance Day

It's Sunday morning and we're sitting in the Manse pew in Portlethen Church waiting for the service to start. There's Stuart in his grey tweed suit and green tartan tie at the end of the row next to the side aisle. Alongside him sits Mum in her fur coat and her navy felt hat with the feather in the brim, her arm around little sister, Sandra, keeping her safe and still. Next to her is Marilyn then me, in our bowler hats and our Sunday best coats with their soft velvet collars. This Sunday, however, there is something different about us - we are all wearing red poppies, because this is Remembrance Sunday. Before we left home this morning, Mum pinned poppies onto the lapels of our coats and told us that this was a special day when we remembered all the people who died in the War and that it would be a sad day for all those who had lost someone they loved.

So I sit waiting for the service to start, stroking my poppy, carefully avoiding the sharp point of the pin, thinking about what Mum said. The trouble is the War ended when I was only three years old and

TO THE GLORIOUS MEMORY OF OUR
1914 FALLEN HEROES. 1918

2ND LIEUT. JAS. MASSON, GORDON HIGHLANDERS
SGT. GEORGE L. DUTHIE, AUSTRALIAN I.F.
SGT. A. D. MARR, M.A. GORDON HIGHLANDERS
L. CORPL. ALEXR CRAIG, " "
PTE. JOHN W. BARRON, " "
PTE. ROBERT CALDER, SHERWOOD FORESTERS
PTE. JOHN CRAIG, GORDON HIGHLANDERS
PTE. JAMES DICK, " "
PTE. GORDON DOUGLAS, " "
PTE. JAMES GAULD, " "
PTE. GEORGE A. GRAY, " "
PTE. JOHN LEIPER, " "
PTE. ALEXR SPENCE, " "
PTE. E. W. TAGGART, " "
PTE. JOHN TAWSE, " "
PTE. WILLIAM WALKER, " "
PTE. JOHN WOOD, " "
PTE. JOHN WOOD, " "
PTE. JOHN CRAIG, SEAFORTH HIGHLANDERS
PTE. R. G. MILNE, " "
PTE. G. DEMPSTER, H.L.I.
ALEXANDER MAIN, R.N.R. (T)
GEORGE WOOD, " "
JOHN WOOD, " "
PTE. GEORGE THOMSON, ROYAL MONTREAL REGT

PTE. PETER HARDIE, GORDON HIGHLANDERS.

Soldiers and sailors from Portlethen and district
killed in the 1914-18 War

I was too young to remember anything. I've heard people saying that I'm a "War baby" and so are Stuart and Marilyn because we were all born during the War. We were lucky that Dad was a minister and didn't get called up to fight in the Army. Perhaps it's just as well because I don't think he'd have been much use as a soldier: he won't kill anything, not a mouse, not a spider, not a wasp. He says,

"They're all God's creatures,"

and shows us how to catch wasps and bees in a tumbler, when they get into the house, and then take them outside and let them fly away. We should be glad that Mum is not quite so particular or the house would be overrun by mice and we'd never have roast chicken for Sunday lunch.

However, Dad did play his part in the War effort, even though he didn't go away to fight. He was chaplain at the RAF station in Portlethen and he worked as a Red Cross driver all through the War. He has told us stories about trying to navigate his way along country roads when all the signposts had been removed so that the Germans, if they came ashore at Aberdeen, would not be able to find their way to London. We heard about the time he had to drive a woman, who was just about to give birth, to the hospital in Aberdeen and he was terrified that they weren't going to make it in time and she was going to have her baby in his car and he would have to be the midwife.

Although I can't remember the War, I can see signs of it all around. We've still got a roll of the material, used to make blackout curtains, propped up against the wall of the washhouse and there's a gasmask hanging on a peg in the cupboard under the stairs. There are concrete blocks at the top of the cliff path down to Portlethen shore and all along the Beach Esplanade in Aberdeen, set there to block the German tanks if they came ashore, and there's a pillbox in the middle of the field near Balquharn, presumably to guard the road south from Aberdeen, though I expect Mr Hitler's Panzer divisions would have made short work of that. The radar pylons still stand on top of the hill at Craighead and Dad goes every week to hold a service at the RAF station. Linda McKay, in my class at school, lives at the other side of the main road in the wooden huts, built to house people bombed out of Aberdeen. When we drive down Nigg Brae towards the River Dee, Dad points out the bungalow on the right hand side of the road which took a direct hit from a bomb and had to be rebuilt and the empty shell of the Ice Rink, near the Bridge of Dee, which was destroyed when a German bomber crash landed on it.

My thoughts are interrupted by the sound of the church bell ringing to mark the start of the service. The door at the back of the church opens and down the aisle walks Maxie Gray, the Beadle, carrying the big black leather Bible. He climbs the steps to the pulpit, sets the Bible down on the lectern and returns to stand at the foot of the steps. In walks Dad in his black gown with the red Glasgow University hood. His head is bowed and he's looking serious and thoughtful, clasping his file of notes for the sermon. He climbs the steps of the pulpit and sits down. Miss Richmond, the organist, gradually brings the music she is playing to a close. There is a moment of silence before Dad stands up and the service begins.

We start as always with a Psalm, this time Psalm 90,

"O God our help in ages past,"

and then Dad reads from the Bible, John, Chapter 15,

"This is my commandment, that you love one another as I have loved you. Greater love hath no man than this, that a man lay down his life for his friends."

As he finishes the reading and closes the Bible, we hear the church bell ringing. Dad asks us all to stand up and says that, on this the 11th hour of the 11th day of the 11th month, we will stand together in silence for two minutes to remember all those who gave their lives in the War so that we might live in freedom.

I stand up, close my eyes and bow my head, concentrating on keeping still and not fidgeting. Time passes slowly. I glance at Mum out of the corner of my eye but she is looking very solemn, holding Sandra close to keep her quiet. I daren't look at Marilyn. She can be such a giggler and that would be a disaster. It seems an awfully long two minutes but, at last, I hear the church bell ringing and there is a general coughing and shuffling of feet as we all sit down and the service continues.

We sing the hymn, "I vow to thee my country," and Dad prays for peace throughout the world. It seems to me a bit of a puzzle that sometimes we are being encouraged to fight and at other times to be peaceful. Sometimes we sing hymns that sound a bit warlike, like "Onward Christian soldiers, marching as to war," and "Stand up, stand up for Jesus, we soldiers of the cross." Are we meant to think that fighting is a good thing? Or should we always remember that our Dad tells us, "We're all God's children," and refuse to hurt anyone, no matter what they do? It's a puzzle. I'll need to ask him.

Anyway, now it's time for the sermon. For a while I listen to what Dad is saying but then my mind drifts back to thinking about the War. I can't remember anything but I've heard lots of stories from people who do remember what it was like. Aunt Lena told us that, one night when she was staying with us on holiday in Portlethen, the siren sounded and they could hear the German bombers flying overhead on their way to bomb the docks in Aberdeen. She said Mum went into our bedroom, picked up Stuart and me out of our cots and brought us down to the small bathroom under the stairs that Dad had chosen as the safest place in the Manse. Mum insisted Aunt Lena got up and came and joined us, saying,

"If we're going to die, then we're all going to die together."

Aunt Lena was a firewatcher near her home in Paisley and was used to watching the bombing of Clydebank, and so she thought it was a fuss about nothing and that it was very unlikely that the

Stuart Dunn being carried by a WRAF (Women's Royal Air Force) officer from the Radar Station at Portlethen

Germans would drop a bomb on Portlethen. Next day, however, Dad heard that in fact two bombs had been dropped on Portlethen. One had fallen on the church brae - it hadn't exploded and was being removed by the bomb disposal men. The other had exploded in a field and killed a cow.

I know we had WRAF (Women's Royal Air Force) officers staying with us all during the War, working at the radar station during the day, sleeping in the attic bedrooms in the Manse at night. I've seen a photo of one lady, dressed in her uniform, holding Stuart as a toddler, and Mum said they were a great help to her looking after us as babies.

Now I hear Dad bringing the sermon to a close and know it's time for the Collection. I burrow in my coat pocket and fish out a threepenny piece ready to drop in the velvet pouch when it is passed along our pew. There is a final hymn, the Benediction and then Dad makes his way slowly down the pulpit steps, along the blue carpet between the pews and out through the doors at the back of the church. The congregation stands up and follows him outside to gather round the War Memorial, its silver-grey granite finger pointing up to the sky from its solid, square base on the hilltop overlooking the fields and farms of Portlethen.

The sky is grey and overcast, dark clouds scudding along in the strong wind. I am standing at the front of the crowd, along with all the other children, holding onto my hat to stop it blowing away, listening to the distant thunder of the waves breaking on the rocks and the call of the seagulls as they wheel above the cliffs at Portlethen shore.

I look up and read the inscription on the stone facing me, the black letters carved into the granite of the War Memorial,

"To the glorious memory of our fallen heroes, 1914-18"

Underneath is the list of those who were killed in that war. So many names and yet we are such a small community. So many familiar names, families who still live locally. I see the name John Barron, the same surname as Yvonne Barron in my class at school. There's John Tawse. I wonder if he is related to Mabel Tawse in my class? There are Alexander Craig and John Craig, perhaps relatives of the Craig family who sit next to us in church. I read the names of their regiments. So many of these young men were serving with the Gordon Highlanders – we pass their barracks at the Bridge of Don every time we drive to the beach at Menie. I run my eye down the list and see that Alexander Main, George Wood and John Wood all died while serving with the Royal Navy Reserve (Trawlers.) Were they local fishermen conscripted into the Navy? Are they relatives of Mr Main and Mr Wood, two of the elders of Portlethen Church?

I can see Dad standing silently, head bowed, his black gown billowing in the wind as he waits for everyone to gather. At last he starts speaking, softly, solemnly,

"They shall not grow old, as we that are left grow old:

Age shall not weary them, nor the years condemn

At the going down of the sun and in the morning

We will remember them."

Dad's voice is very sad and wobbly. He sounds like he is going to cry. I watch him anxiously. Is he remembering his own father, who left his wife and five year old son behind to go and fight in the trenches in the First World War in France, and how he was badly wounded and nearly died? Or is he thinking of the young farmers and fishermen from Portlethen and Findon and Downies named on the War Memorial and feeling what it must be like for their families? I hear the sound of a woman sobbing quietly in the crowd of people behind me and feel like crying myself. I look at Stuart. In a few years time he will be old enough to be called up to do his National Service. Will he have to go and fight somewhere? What if gets killed and his name ends up on this War Memorial and that he doesn't "grow old as we who are left grow old?"

I watch as Billy Main, dressed in his Army uniform, steps forward and lays a wreath of red poppies at the foot of the War Memorial. There is a moment of silence and then the crunch of gravel as Dad turns away and walks slowly back into the church. I watch him go.

Mum gathers us all together and we walk down the church brae and along the road back to The Manse. Somehow, today, there is no running and chasing each other as we usually do on the way home from church. There is no laughing or chattering, no throwing our bowler hats in the air. This morning, we walk home together quietly.

# December

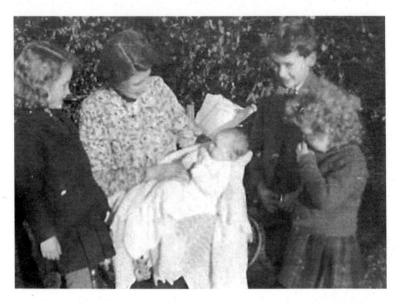

Elizabeth, Mrs Florence Dunn, baby Sandra, Stuart and Marilyn

# Our Little Sister

There is a dark shadow hanging over our house. Everything is grey and gloomy, with whispers and hushed voices, and faces lined with worry and anxiety. It's nearly Christmas but there is no joy in this house. Everywhere is quiet: there's no laughing and teasing, no shouting and squabbling, no banging doors or noisy footsteps clattering down the stairs. There's no Dad singing cheerfully along with "Sing Something Simple" on the radio. There's no Mum bustling around the kitchen, telling us to take off our muddy shoes, or drink up our milk because it's rich in calcium. Even Magnus, our little dog, is subdued, curled up quietly on the armchair by the fire.

Our baby sister, Sandra, is very ill with pneumonia. Dad has dismantled her cot, carried it downstairs and set it up in the drawing room, and we see him going in and out with armloads of peat, keeping the fire burning day and night. Mum has brought a quilt and a pillow downstairs and is sleeping on the couch. The curtains are drawn and Mum spends all day sitting in the firelight by the cot, stroking the baby's head, willing her to get well again.

Me and Stuart and Marilyn huddle together on the stairs, listening for the knock on the back door, and the footsteps as Dad leads Dr Horne through the hall and into the drawing room. We're all feeling sad but I'm even more miserable than the others because I have a guilty conscience. I know in my heart that I haven't always felt kindly towards our baby sister or been good to her.

I remember the night she was born, being wakened by footsteps on the stairs, the voices of Dad and Dr Horne in the hallway outside my bedroom, and then the sound of a baby crying. A few moments later, my door creaked open and there was Dad whispering,

"Elizabeth, are you awake? Would you like to come and see Mummy's new dolly?"

He picked me up and carried me through into the front bedroom, and there was Mum, sitting propped up with lots of pillows, cuddling a baby, with a mop of dark hair, not fair and curly like me and Marilyn. I looked at this new baby with suspicion and said,

"It's not a dolly. It's a golly."

Mum and Dad laughed. They seemed to be surprisingly happy with this dark-haired baby, even though she didn't look like the rest of us.

"This is your new baby sister," said Mum, smiling at me. "Her name is Alexandra Florence, Alexandra after your Dad, Florence after me, but we're going to call her Sandra for short."

I remember thinking to myself,

"What's so special about this baby that she's being called after Mum and Dad? None of the rest of us were. Me and Stuart were named after grandparents. Marilyn's name was chosen by our Great Aunts."

It seems to me that, ever since that night when Sandra was born, my life has changed for the worse. When I come home from school, there's Mum in the kitchen, sitting in the chair by the fire with Sandra on her knee, making funny faces, talking silly baby talk, and Marilyn playing happily on the rug at her feet, cuddling her doll, pretending it's her baby. Mum looks up when I come in and smiles.

"Hello, darling. How was school today?" she asks but, just as I'm about to tell her that I can now write my name and am learning my two times table, she says,

"Will you pass me the baby's shawl, and can you keep an eye on Marilyn for a minute while I put Sandra down for a nap?"

Ever since Sandra was born, Mum doesn't have time to listen to me, just keeps asking me to do a lot of things I don't really want to do. When I complain, Mum says,

"Elizabeth, you're my oldest daughter. I need you to help me."

"But what about Stuart?" I protest.

"He's a boy," says Mum, as Stuart comes home from school, dumps his schoolbag and rushes off to play football. It's not fair. I know Mum grew up on a farm where the boys worked in the fields with their father and the girls helped their mother with housework and looking after the younger children. It's what Mum is used to, but I still don't think it's right.

So now I'm sitting on the stairs with Stuart and Marilyn remembering how fed up I was and blaming the baby for everything, but now feeling guilty because she's ill and wishing I had been kinder to her.

We hear Dad coming out of the drawing room, closing the door gently behind him, then his footsteps starting to climb the stairs. He smiles when he sees us and holds out his hand.

"Come on. Let's get you all to bed," he says.

"Is Sandra going to be alright?" asks Stuart.

"Of course," says Dad, reassuringly. "Don't worry. Dr Horne is the best doctor in the world, and you know your Mum was a nurse in a

Florence Dunn in her nurses's uniform

Marilyn holding baby Sandra

children's hospital before you were born. She's had lots of practice at looking after babies when they're ill."

Dad helps us wash our face and hands, brush our teeth and put on our pyjamas. He sits on the side of the bed as me and Marilyn cuddle down under the blankets. We fold our hands together, close our eyes and Dad listens as we say our prayers,

"In my little bed I lie

Heavenly father hear my cry

Lord protect me through the night

And keep me safe till morning light.

God bless Mummy, Daddy, Stuart, Elizabeth, Marilyn and Sandra. Amen"

Dad says, "Night Night," as he leaves, and I think of all the other evenings when Mum put us to bed, tucking us in, laughing, whispering,

"Good Night. Sleep tight. Don't let the bugs bite."

I lie in the dark, worrying about the baby downstairs who is so ill, remembering something I did one day, something I wish I hadn't done.

That day, I'd come back from school as usual, glad to be home, wanting to go and play, but as soon as I came into the kitchen, Mum said,

"Elizabeth, I need to peel the potatoes and get the dinner on. Will you push Sandra in the pram up and down the front path for me and see if you can get her off to sleep?"

I wanted to stamp my feet and shout,

"No, I don't want to. I've spent all day at school sitting still, doing what I was told. I want to go outside and have a swing and lean back and stretch my feet out till I can see over the hedge. I want to skip and skip till I count up to a hundred, and bounce my ball against the wall. I do not want to look after a crying baby."

I flung my schoolbag down on the floor, scowling, muttering

under my breath. I grabbed the handle of the pram, pushing it roughly through the hall, bouncing it over the front doorstep, almost scraping the door jamb. I knew I should be turning to walk slowly up the path to the gate and back again, but instead, I gritted my teeth and pushed the pram with all my might, straight ahead, hurling it as far away from me as possible. I watched it fly across the gravel, heard the bump as the front wheels hit the edge of the lawn, and the crash as over it went, toppling headfirst, back wheels spinning in the air. Out tumbled the baby on to the grass in a tangle of sheets and blankets, howling with fright. I froze for a moment, shocked, horrified at what I'd done, then turned and ran back through the front door into the kitchen.

"Sandra's fallen out of the pram," I screamed. Mum dropped the potato she was peeling, raced out through the hall, into the garden. She lifted up the baby, cradling her up over her shoulder, patting her back, rocking her, soothing her, murmuring to her till her sobs quietened. I pulled the pram upright, picked up the blankets, not daring to look at Mum, muttering,

"I'm sorry. I'm sorry."

"It's alright," said Mum. "I'm sure it was an accident."

She laid Sandra down on the mattress, tucked the blankets firmly round her, rocking the pram to and fro till the baby was asleep. Then she went back into the house, back to her potato peeling, leaving me standing on the path, staring at the ground, scuffing my feet on the gravel, feeling very guilty.

Now here I am lying in bed, thinking about my baby sister so ill downstairs, remembering how unkind I was, wishing I could take it back, knowing now that, even though she is new and very small, she is already part of this family and none of us will ever be happy again if anything bad happens to her. I cry myself to sleep.

Next morning I wake to the sound of the radio drifting up the stairs from the kitchen. I look across at Marilyn's curly head in the bed opposite and see sleepy eyes looking back at me. We lie quietly and listen. We can tell something is different. We sit bolt upright, scramble out of bed and run downstairs. Dad is in the kitchen, stirring the porridge pot on the cooker. Stuart is there, playing with Magnus, pulling his ears, tickling his tummy. The little dog is lying on his back with his legs in the air, wriggling with contentment. Dad turns and smiles at us.

"Your little sister is much better today. She's going to be fine," he says.

What a relief! Me and Marilyn laugh and hug each other and dance around the kitchen table. Magnus jumps up and runs to join us, barking with excitement, tail wagging furiously.

"I'm just going to see if your Mum would like some breakfast," says Dad. "Do you want to come with me? You'll need to be very quiet because the baby's sleeping."

We tiptoe through the hall and into the drawing room. The curtains are open and sunlight is streaming in through the bay window. A fire glows in the hearth and next to it is the baby's cot. Mum is sitting on an upright chair keeping watch but she turns as we come in, holding out her arms. Marilyn runs to her and Mum lifts her on to her knee and cuddles her. We've all missed Mum being around all the time but Marilyn most of all because she's the youngest. Me and Stuart creep round the other side of the cot and peer in through the bars. We look at the tiny baby, so pale and fragile.

"She's over the worst," says Mum, "But I'll need you all to help me look after her for a day or two until she's completely well again."

We nod solemnly, pleased to be asked to help look after our little sister.

Mum stands up, holding Marilyn by the hand.

"Right, let's go to the kitchen and see what's for breakfast."

She smiles at me and says,

"Elizabeth, I would like you to stay with Sandra just for a minute. I'll leave the door a little bit open and call me if she wakes up. You can sit in my chair and be her nurse."

Everyone goes out and I'm left sitting on the chair by the cot, watching my little sister, listening to her gentle breathing. I reach out a hand through the bars and stroke her soft silky hair, whispering to her,

"I'm sorry I didn't like your dark hair. I'm sorry I thought you were a nuisance. I'm sorry I tipped you out of the pram. I promise that from now on I'll always take care of you and I'll never ever be cross with you again."

I see my little sister smile in her sleep and know that she has forgiven me.

# Postscript

Children growing up in post-war Britain were expected to accept the rules of the community around them, the school they attended and the family they were born into.

I never saw a policeman in Portlethen when I was a child, and yet we knew we had to be law-abiding and well behaved wherever we went in the village.

At school, we were taught to value hardwork, perseverance, and discipline. There was lots of learning of facts, of repetition and practice, very little emphasis on creativity or self-expression and, certainly, no suggestion that learning could be fun.

At home, we children of The Manse were taught to be honest and always tell the truth, to be unselfish and think of others, to pull our weight for the good of the family, to be kind to each other and to the animals and birds around us, to be cheerful and uncomplaining and to always do what we were told without arguments.

Even today, some children seem to find it easy to be good and always obey the rules. Others, like me as a child, find it more difficult. I remember childhood as a struggle between trying to please others and wanting to please myself, between doing what I was told and doing what I wanted. Sometimes, I felt like one of life's buttercups, swaying gently in the breeze, happily shining golden-yellow among the other wild flowers in the meadow. At other times, I felt as wayward and stubborn and prickly as a bramble.

Fortunately, this was a time when both buttercups and brambles could find a place and flourish in the fields and hedgerows of Portlethen. Let's hope it's the same today.

# Appendix 1

Christine De Luca is one of the foremost contemporary poets in Scotland. Her work has appeared in journals worldwide and she has read at many literary festivals. She is the author of the poem, "The Morning After," which was recited on television by Scotland's young voters ahead of the Referendum in 2014. She is currently the Edinburgh Makar- the poet laureate for the City of Edinburgh.

Our family has known Christine since she was a child, as one of the Pearson family who came down from Shetland every summer to spend a holiday with us at The Manse in Portlethen. The friendship between her parents and ours lasted a lifetime, and the relationship between our families has continued into the next generation. Joy Pearson, now Joy Goodlad, still lives in Shetland and visits Marilyn whenever she comes south to Aberdeen. Christine and I meet whenever I am in Edinburgh, and we enjoy the opportunity to catch up with family news and remember old times.

"Pilgrim to Portlethen" is a poem, written by Christine De Luca, in her book of poetry titled "Plain Song," published by The Shetland Library in 2002.

# Pilgrim to Portlethen

*Holiday snapshot*

Portlethen was a solid village rooted
between cliff and moor where words
like 'future', 'past' seemed arbitrary.

For us on holiday it was mildest magic.
Mothers cooking, catching up.
Fathers with indulgent cars full
of comparisons of beaches, fair rides.

Mid July in the warm room at night, savouring
the muffle of distant trains. Even now
one at that time, that distance, and I am there
happy among four or five small beds
full of long and secret whispering
when we thought the day had stopped
because we had.

*Ticket to ride*

Here were buses we had never seen before
never dreamed of: double-deckers built
to impress, with a list of places to traverse
and a conductress who could slickly punch
a colour-coded ticket without looking
flick change into compartments of a pouch.
With her criss-cross leather straps
and snappy hat, this was a job to covet.

That would have been enough
but a ticket and a train journey
to Stonehaven and back
was like riding to the stars.
And hours and hours were spent
on the bridge above the railway line
to stalk a big train, hear it far off
listen as its single thread of sound
unravelled; would hold our breath
as it thundered underneath
dash across to count carriages
watch it as it tilted out of sight
pulling a plait of sounds
tightly as it went.


*Return*

The family has gone now, as ours
grown, scattered, made new alliances.
The oil boom has exploded myths
of timelessness. Superstores encamp
and factories have arrived
from distant drawing boards.
The rail-bridge arches its apology
across the line, looks out of scale.
It seems incongruous that guards
on inter-city trains announce
its imminence. For me, returning
is a pilgrimage of mind and heart.
I speak happily in past tenses
gentle syntax of so many futures.

# Appendix 2

Primary 1 and 2 at Portlethen Primary School, 1947 (see page 18)

**Teacher**: Miss Duncan

**Back Row**: Ian Third, James McKandie, Derek Crighton, not known, Peter Diack, Derek Craig, Stuart Dunn, Alasdair Grant, Sandy Burnett

**Third Row**: Elizabeth Dunn, Sheena Crockett, Margaret McKandie, Isabella Sinclair, Isobel Jeffray, Barbara Moir, Violet Michael, Elena Melvin, Hazel Mann, Linda McKay

**Second Row**: David Hutcheon, not known, Alma McGibbon, Nessie Patterson, Yvonne Barron, Iris Mitchell, ? Lawrence, Eileen Shand, Joyce Forbes, Margaret Stratton, Kathleen Milne, Adeline Masson, Mabel Tawse, not known

**Front Row**: ? Mitchell, George Lawrence, David Reid, James McGregor, Billy Brown, Sandy Moir, James Moir, Sandy Milne